GROW YOUR SOUL

40-day guide to get
unstuck, restored, and reset
in faith, church, and spirit

Mike Acker

GROW YOUR SOUL: A 40-Day Guide to Get Unstuck, Restored, and Reset in Faith, Church, and Spirit

Copyright ©2020, Mike Acker

All rights reserved. No part of this publication may be reproduced, stored in a retrieval system, or transmitted in any form or by an means—electronic, mechanical, photocopy, recording, or any other—except for brief quotations in printed reviews, without the prior permission of the author.

Unless otherwise indicated, all Scripture quotations are taken from the Holy Bible, New Living Translation, copyright 1996, 2004. Used by permission of Tyndale House Publishers, Inc., Wheaton, Illinois 60189. All rights reserved.

Additional Scripture taken from the HOLY BIBLE, NEW INTERNATIONAL VERSION®. Copyright © 1973, 1978, 1984 Biblica. Used by permission of Zondervan. All rights reserved.
Some names and identifying details have been changed to protect the privacy of individuals.

Printed in the United States of America
ISBN: 978-1-7349756-1-1

Requests for information should be addressed to:
Mike Acker, 113 Cherry St #35754, Seattle WA 98104

Contents

INTRODUCTION: "I DON'T WANT TO GO TO CHURCH." 5

week ONE: GROW BACKWARDS 13
- GROW BACKWARDS: **day ONE** 15
- GROW BACKWARDS: **day TWO** 20
- GROW BACKWARDS: **day THREE** 26
- GROW BACKWARDS: **day FOUR** 31
- GROW BACKWARDS: **day FIVE** 35

week TWO: GROW FORWARDS 41
- GROW FORWARDS: **day ONE** 43
- GROW FORWARDS: **day TWO** 48
- GROW FORWARDS: **day THREE** 57
- GROW FORWARDS: **day FOUR** 63
- GROW FORWARDS: **day FIVE** 68

week THREE: GROW WITHWARDS 75
- GROW WITHWARDS: **day ONE** 77
- GROW WITHWARDS: **day TWO** 82
- GROW WITHWARDS: **day THREE** 87
- GROW WITHWARDS: **day FOUR** 92
- GROW WITHWARDS: **day FIVE** 98

week FOUR: GROW INWARDS 103
- GROW INWARDS: **day ONE** 105
- GROW INWARDS: **day TWO** 110
- GROW INWARDS: **day THREE** 116
- GROW INWARDS: **day FOUR** 121
- GROW INWARDS: **day FIVE** 126

week FIVE: GROW OUTWARDS 133
- GROW OUTWARDS: day **ONE** 135
- GROW OUTWARDS: day **TWO** 142
- GROW OUTWARDS: day **THREE** 147
- GROW OUTWARDS: day **FOUR** 152
- GROW OUTWARDS: day **FIVE** 156

week SIX: GROW UPWARDS 161
- GROW UPWARDS: day **ONE** 163
- GROW UPWARDS: day **TWO** 169
- GROW UPWARDS: day **THREE** 173
- GROW UPWARDS: day **FOUR** 178
- GROW UPWARDS: day **FIVE** 183

week SEVEN: GROW DOWNWARDS 189
- GROW DOWNWARDS: day **ONE** 191
- GROW DOWNWARDS: day **TWO** 196
- GROW DOWNWARDS: day **THREE** 201
- GROW DOWNWARDS: day **FOUR** 206
- GROW DOWNWARDS: day **FIVE** 212

week EIGHT: GROW TOWARDS JESUS 217
- GROW TOWARDS JESUS: day **ONE** 219
- GROW TOWARDS JESUS: day **TWO** 224
- GROW TOWARDS JESUS: day **THREE** 228
- GROW TOWARDS JESUS: day **FOUR** 232
- GROW TOWARDS JESUS: day **FIVE** 239

CONCLUSION: "I WILL TAKE MY NEXT STEP." .. 245

ACKNOWLEDGEMENTS 253
ABOUT MIKE ACKER 255

INTRODUCTION:
"I DON'T WANT TO GO TO CHURCH."

"I don't want to go to church…"

"In fact, I don't know if I will ever want to go."

Those quotes might not sound bizarre. After all, church participation continues to drop all across the Unites States along with other western countries. However, this time, these words were coming from someone who had been a pastor for well over a decade.

Those were *my* words.

That is how I felt.

I was tired, hurt, frustrated, burned out, and stuck. Outwardly, I was in shape, but on the inside, my soul was sucked dry.

Can *you* relate?

Have *you* been hurt by the 'church'? Does *your* soul feel weary? Do *you* wonder at the value of attending a service? Do *you* feel fake, stagnant, or apathetic? I can relate. That is how I felt.

With this book, my goal is to give you some of the same help that came to me. My goal is to help you grow again, not so you can be like you used to be, but so that you can become more like who God intended you to be.

WHAT THIS BOOK *IS NOT*

This book does not have all the answers.

This book does not tell you to quit the Church and give up on faith.

This book does not blame others.

And this book is not the story of how I got to the place where my soul was tired. After all, you have your own story and I have mine. Instead, this is my story of how I believe God has led (and continues to lead) me out of that soul tiredness.

As I write these words, I am not working in a church, but I do participate in a church. I am not the Christian I used to be, but I am a Christian who has learned a lot of grace and empathy. I am not the perfect example of Jesus, but I do try to lead my family to become more like Jesus. In fact, after being a pastoral intern, a pastoral student, a staff pastor, a church planter, a lead pastor, and a pastor of pastors for over two decades, I am not a lot of what I thought I was. I don't have all the answers (it turns out I never did). I'm not the ideal Christian leader (I found out I never was).

There is a lot that this book and this author are *not*. But who I am becoming, I share with you. Together, we can journey towards Jesus, and as we do, we can see our souls grow healthier, more whole, and even *holy*.

In just a minute, let's unpack that word *holy*. But before we get too far… there were some other writings that I put together to help people, but it didn't fit here. If you would like that go to: https://book.mikeacker.com/grow.

HOLY?

Did you know God has called those who follow him to be *holy*!? Jesus clearly stated this exact sentiment when he said to his followers *"Be holy…"* (**Lev 11:44, Matt 5:48**) So what does that really mean?

"Oh no… Does it mean I have to try harder!? Is this going to make me even more tired?"

Read on.

The word *holy* holds the notion of separateness. So, what are we to be separate from? From certain kinds of people? No; after all, Jesus moved and walked among all types of people. Are we simply meant to be more moral? No, Jesus rebuked people who merely tried to live moral lives.

Jesus called his followers then, and calls us now, to be set apart *for* God. Jesus invites us into a sacred way of life where we see life as God sees life, where we love as God loves, and where we actually become like God at the core of who we are: our soul. This is a place of significance, wholeness, and rest.

I hope you find this word refreshing. God wants to guide you to holiness from the inside out. There are many words that come to mind when people think about Christians and the church:

believers, political, hypocrites, good people, big buildings, budgets, mission trips, compassionate, business, moral, phobic, and the list goes on with both good and bad descriptions.

But what word does God use? Holy.

How can we do that?

It doesn't happen in an instant. That's for sure! I've been a Christian for quite a while; I've been on this path of healing for a while, and God is still working in me and on me.

There is no single formula, either. We can't do it by simply praying for it, going to church, or trying real hard. So how?

We must choose to say *yes*. Yes, to God. Yes, to his life. Yes, to patience. Yes, to growth. God wants our soul to grow. We get to choose to grow healthy, whole, and holy or to stay stagnant, stuck, and hurt.

You don't have to stay down. It's okay to get back up. This book can help you.

Together, let's take next steps that lead to new levels. And let's not just grow in one area. Growth is more holistic than that.

Our soul grows in more than one direction.

WHAT THIS BOOK *IS*

I had stopped reading the Bible and spending time in prayer. I even skipped several Sundays, but ultimately, my wife and I brought our son to church and we sat quietly in the seats. When it was over, we made our way out the door quietly. I was too tired to do anything else.

> *"Go back and do the things you did at first."*
>
> **—Jesus**

Then I heard those words from Jesus. I didn't *hear* them. The words just popped in my head. So, what did I do at *first*? I recalled the greatest highlights of my faith journey. What did I do when I first dove into following Jesus? I gave my clothes away on the streets of Seattle at 2am. I confessed my sin to a new friend in Boston. I fasted from eating for three weeks.

Why did I do those things? Because during those times, there was nothing more I wanted than to know God and be close to God. Driven by a desire to be *holy* like God, I chose to participate in ancient disciplines, which increased my connection to God. That is what I did at *first*.

One more thing came to mind. During one of my greatest seasons of faith, I wrote 40 days' worth of devotional readings intended for the church that I lead.

> *"Go back and do the things you did at first."*
>
> **—Jesus**

I pulled out the readings and re-read them. My soul stirred. I began to reflect on what I had written long ago. I began to act.

As my soul continues to mend, heal, and grow, I now share my journey and my book with you.

I've edited and formatted the book that I wrote many years ago so you can read what I am reading. I divided the content into eight weeks of daily readings. There are five readings per week. Each reading has a page for notes or for writing down personal actions to take. The five daily readings consist of spiritual truths illustrated through anecdotes, stories, and scriptures.

I've organized it to be read in eight weeks, but don't make your goal to stick to a rigid schedule; use it to re-engage your soul with God. The first seven weeks are seven disciplines that point you to become more like God at the level of the soul. The eighth week is full of reflections designed to get you focused on Jesus.

Depending on your background, experience, and previous studies, you may or may not learn something brand new with each reading. New information is not the point. Often, Christians will use the word "deep" to mean acquiring some new information. True depth is not learning something new. Depth is acting on what you learn. Use this book to act on what you have learned and what you are learning.

You can choose to skip to a discipline you want to practice. Or, take a couple weeks to focus on one discipline. You might find it helpful to do this as a group, with a friend, or even as a church. I do not intend this to be an exhaustive list of all Christian disciplines, but it's where I re-started, and I invite you to join me.

As you put these into practice, you *will* grow. I know this because, yes, the Bible teaches it and I've seen it in others.

More personally, I know this work because I see it working in me.

Another verse from the Bible came to mind in this weary season of the soul:

"I am confident of this. That Jesus who began a good work in you will carry it on to completion."–Paul, the Apostle

IF YOU ARE HURTING

Friend,

God is not done with you.

I'm sorry you have gone through whatever it is you went through. I'm sorry they did what they did. Or, I'm sorry you did what you did. I'm sorry life took the turn it did.

It's not fun. It hurts. But it happened, and it doesn't just go away.

I'm sorry you are tired. I feel your pain. My tiredness caused my heart to ache. It was an ugly season of my soul.

I hope that you join me and find this book to be a gentle, good, and even fun guide. I pray you will begin to take your next steps to grow towards God. Here's what will happen: as you take your next step and the step after that, you will see how exterior action leads to interior transformation. It won't be quick or simple. You may even take steps back.

But over time, you will look back on the steps you take today and see that, even in the midst of the current reality, you are growing your soul to become more like God.

week ONE: GROW BACKWARDS

Traveling in this direction is not living in the past, wishing we were in a different time of our life or becoming like we used to be. GROWING BACKWARDS brings us to the discipline of **examination**. It's knowing our minds and making space for our thoughts. It's learning from the past so that we may grow in the present.

GROW BACKWARDS   day ONE

SOCRATES

Socrates, the Greek philosopher, is still known for his enduring wisdom and for making people think.

As I've read some of his dialogue with his student, Plato, I've found myself questioning motives, beliefs, and actions, as well as social agendas, governing structure and conventional wisdom. Other times I have found my eyes reading while my mind goes blank. When my mind meets back up with my eyes, I realize that I am thinking, "Huh?"

Nonetheless, Socrates makes me think. One of his famous quotes has stayed in my mind for many years: ὁ δὲ ἀνεξέταστος βίος οὐ βιωτὸς ἀνθρώπῳ. In English, "the unexamined life is not worth living for a human being."

Socrates believed this with his whole being. He ended up dying for this belief. As a philosopher and teacher, Socrates made people question. He made them question their thinking. He made them question their way of doing things. He made them question their purpose. He didn't do this to lead them to confusion; he did this to lead them to clarity. He desired that people live lives of meaning and purpose instead of mediocrity and apathy.

Eventually, Socrates was put on trial for disrupting the peace of the city by causing them to question the conventions of society. He was charged with heresy and was given a choice: be exiled away from Athens where he exercised his examinations, or die.

It is in this setting that Socrates is known for the famous quote. Socrates chose death.

I assume that Socrates felt that in exile, he wouldn't have had the ability to dialogue with people in such a way as to learn the answers to his many questions. He felt that he would have to give up his examination of the soul.

How seriously do you take the examination of your soul?

When was the last time you took a walk to work through the winding alleys of your mind? When was the last time you sat down and worked through your doubts, your fears, your questions, and your concerns?

Take a moment and search Socrates' quote. You will find the saying in Wiki quotes, you will find the history in Wikipedia, and you will find commentary in endless blogs. It *seems* that many people have chosen to act out Socrates' words. It *appears* that many amateur authors are working through their questions. It *looks* like examination is a common practice.

Read on.

Many of the blogs are the true internal wrestling and workings of the mind. Examination.

Many more are mere surface thoughts presented for the world to see their wit. Such blogs are mindlessly presented to gain popularity from a population who would rather read surface thoughts of another than delve into the deep of their own psyche. Entertainment.

Which are you? Do you examine your soul? Or simply amuse yourself?

There is a time for entertainment, but don't let it consume you. Life must be more than mere amusement. Make time to consider your actions, thoughts and feelings. Create time to examine the state of your soul.

Are you aware of God's presence in your life?

Have you given thought to how you stand with your friends and family?

Are you bottling up feelings and emotions?

Have you invited God into your interior?

> *Search me, O God, and know my heart;*
> *test me and know my anxious thoughts.*
>
> *See if there is any offensive way in me,*
> *and lead me in the way everlasting.*
>
> **—Psalms 139:23-24**

ACTION:

Take a moment to reread **Psalms 139:23-24**. *Pray it and invite God to examine your life. Invite Him to reveal areas He is leading you to change. Ask Him to guide you in His path.*

MY THOUGHTS / PLAN OF ACTION

_____
_____
_____
_____
_____
_____
_____
_____
_____
_____
_____
_____

TODAY'S DATE

_____

GROW BACKWARDS day **TWO**

POETRY OF THE SOUL

When was the last time you wrote a poem?

In the 9th grade, I wrote lots of poetry. Some of it was frivolous nonsense that embarrasses me when I re-read it today. Other poems were straight from the soul.

There I was in high school, in the midst of teenage insecurities, changing friendships, and… girls. I had a lot to think about. Somehow, I ended up putting my confusion on paper in the form of poems.

At first, I was proud: "Now I can be like Pearl Jam!"

Then, I was embarrassed: "I do *soccer*–not poetry."

Eventually, I was relieved "I've found a way to work out what is going on inside of me."

Do you have a way to work out what is going on inside of you? Do you have a way to examine your life?

I've listened to several sermons. I've read lots of books. I've perused many magazines. Counsel is so often given through these mediums. *Sometimes,* the advice is presented in the form of a few easy steps; the goal is some amazing life change.

1st Step—Simply take a moment to breathe.

2nd Step—Pray these three sentences.

3rd Step—Believe it.

Completed. "You have arrived *(if you did it right)*—You have one brand new huge home, two new luxury cars and three kids who will never rebel. And if that is not enough, then you will never be depressed and never have fights with your family!"

3 easy steps. Is that all our soul really needs? Is our soul simpler than putting together IKEA furniture? Can problems and tensions we have wrestled with for years be done away with in moments?

My father and I were in a museum of Irish writers in Dublin, Ireland. Walking through the rooms, we read snatches of lyrics. We listened to commentary about the authors' lives. Along the way, we talked. My father majored in British Literature. I like to read it. There was a lot to talk about.

"Mike, I find there to be more truth in many poems than there are in many sermons."

His words caught me off guard. I am a preacher. I write sermons. I preach sermons. It's what I do.

"In a poem, the writer wrestles with life; sometimes it comes out beautifully, and often, it doesn't. So many sermons give you simple steps, as if that is going to do anything."

Whoa, whoa, whoa! I have preached sermons with easy steps. Sometimes all we need are a couple of steps. What's wrong with steps?

I don't think my father had anything against steps. But I do think he was right. If we aren't careful, we can take the truth of our lives and mix it with the truth of the Bible and end up with a simple religious formula to make us feel better for the moment… while never dealing with the tension in our soul.

Where do you process the changing world around you? Where do you wrestle with the tension? Do you even try to wrestle with tension? Or do you just settle for steps?

Is God just or is He merciful? Tension.

Does God choose you or do you choose God? Tension.

Are you fully a Democrat or completely a Republican? Political tension.

Is it right to be pro-life? What about if the mother *will* die? Lots of tension.

Are you Calvinist or Armenian? Theological tension.

Do we get raptured or does God keep us here to redeem this world? Eschatological tension.

Can I be active sexually *(just a little bit even)* before marriage or should I wait until someday when I get married? Sexual tension.

Do I wait for them to come to me or do I go talk to them? Personal tension.

These are BIG areas of life. I could continue for pages with situations saturated with tension. Some would be slightly easier to determine. Others are tauter than tightropes.

There is so much wrestling going on in these areas. Can we really solve all of them with 3 steps?

Consider **Psalms 22** or **Psalms 5**. Pick up a Bible or go online and read it. Here is a man of faith wrestling with God. You can't turn it into 3 steps and an answer. It's poetry. It's tension. It's truth.

Have you simplified your soul and now you know all the answers? It's time to ask some questions. It's time to ask why? It's time to rediscover wonder.

Don't be afraid that you don't know all the answers. You don't. So stop pretending that you do.

It's okay to live in the tension. It's okay to have faith in a God beyond your full comprehension.

Read the **Psalms**. Read the book of **Job**. Read **Ecclesiastes**. These are men of faith. They don't have all the answers.

They admit it. They say it.

> **Job 40:3** (Job responding to God)
>
> (God) You asked, 'Who is this that obscures my counsel without knowledge?'
>
> Surely I spoke of things I did not understand, things too wonderful for me to know.

These Biblical poets have questions, doubts and even confusion. They live in the tension.

And that is okay.

REFLECTION:

What are some areas you wrestle with? Do you have some honest struggles with God? What are they?

MY THOUGHTS / PLAN OF ACTION

_____
_____
_____
_____
_____
_____
_____
_____
_____
_____

TODAY'S DATE

_____

GROW BACKWARDS day THREE

SILLY ISRAELITES

As a kid I was introduced to the Bible. Actually, it was the picture Bible. It took the stories and texts of the Old and New Testament and turned it into a comic-book narrative. I loved reading my Bible. I loved the stories… especially the story of the Israelites in the books of Joshua and Judges.

I found *these* stories comical.

God had completely revealed His power to the Israelites. They had seen God do incredible acts of power. The Israelites had seen God part the Red Sea. They had heard God speak through thunder. They had felt the heat of God's presence in a pillar of fire. These people had experienced God.

Then they forgot.

Throughout the historical accounts of Joshua and Judges, the Israelites would follow God, then they would forget. Life would get rough. So, the Israelites would follow God through the rough season. Then they would forget God again. Life would get rough. The Israelites would follow God and then forget…

Silly Israelites.

As a kid reading my comic book Bible, I would get so frustrated with these fickle people. Who could ever forget what God had done for them? Who could ever forget that God wanted the best for them? Why didn't they just learn from their mistakes?

As an adult reading my picture-less Bible, I can get so frustrated with myself… because I am just like those people.

I forget what God has done for me.

I forget that God actually wants what is best.

I forget to learn from my mistakes.

I find myself asking, "Why did I do this again?" "God, don't you care about me right now?" "How can I keep repeating this sin?" "Why can't I just keep my mouth closed?" "Where are you, God?"

My guess is that you have found yourself being just as silly. You have found yourself repeating the same mistakes. You have found yourself asking the same questions, questions that have already been answered.

The Israelites were forgetful people. So are you and I.

Traveling BACKWARDS through our memories, through our choices and through our questions brings us to a place where we can gain wisdom from experiences. As we think through our past, we can find ourselves more secure in the present. We do not have to redo it all again.

I don't journal every day; maybe I should, but I don't. Yet, I often journal when it counts. I've journaled when I felt like a failure. I've journaled when I've accomplished something great. I've journaled when I've had an experience with God that I never wanted to forget. I've journaled prayers for people. I've journaled petitions, requests and questions. These moments caught on paper have become a way for me to learn from the past. These thin pieces of paper anchor me in God's continual presence even when the currents of my life run rapid.

What anchors you in God's presence? What keeps you from forgetting? What helps you gain wisdom from experiences?

Joshua, one of Israel's wise leaders, chose twelve large stones to be his anchor in the reality of God's provision. God had miraculously led his entire people through the currents of the Jordan River, and Joshua wanted them to remember:

> *When the whole nation had finished crossing the Jordan, the LORD said to Joshua, "Choose twelve men from among the people, one from each tribe, and tell them to take up twelve stones from the middle of the Jordan from right where the priests stood and to carry them over with you and put them down at the place where you stay tonight."*
>
> *So Joshua called together the twelve men he had appointed from the Israelites, one from each tribe, and said to them, "Go over before the ark of the LORD your God into the middle of the Jordan. Each of you is to take up a stone on his shoulder, according to the number of the tribes of the Israelites, to serve as a sign among you. In the future, when your children ask you, 'What do these stones mean?' tell them that the flow of the Jordan was cut off before the ark of the covenant of the LORD.*

When it crossed the Jordan, the waters of the Jordan were cut off. These stones are to be a memorial to the people of Israel forever."

—Joshua 4:1-7

Joshua chose twelve stones. I chose pen and paper. It doesn't matter what you choose. Just choose to remember and stop being silly...

REMEMBER:

What are some of the highlights of your spiritual journey? When did you feel closest to God and why was that?

MY THOUGHTS / PLAN OF ACTION

_____

_____

_____

_____

_____

_____

_____

_____

_____

_____

TODAY'S DATE

_____

GROW BACKWARDS   day FOUR

BRITNEY DID IT AGAIN

The pop star sang her prophecy, "Oops, I did it again." She fell from her height of stardom in 2004. Only to rise again. After a couple years she did it again…

What is it that causes us to do the same wrong thing over and over again? On a macro level, the answer is sin:

> … I am unspiritual, sold as a slave to sin. I do not understand what I do. For what I want to do I do not do, but what I hate I do. And if I do what I do not want to do, I agree that the law is good. As it is, it is no longer I myself who do it, but it is sin living in me…
>
> **—Romans 7: 14b–17**

On a micro level, could it be that we return to our folly because we think we can change without having to actually change our routine?

Albert Einstein defined insanity as "doing the same thing over and over again and expecting different results."

You and I might be insane.

Not all the time. Not every person to the same degree. But insane, nonetheless.

Oh... we want to change, we want to grow to become like God. We want to put to death the sin that remains in us. Jesus has conquered sin. We know that. We want to live it. We want to become more loving, patient, kind and generous people. We want to... but do we? Or do we keep doing the same thing over and over again... hoping, wishing and wanting but never changing...

Without changing what we do, we don't change who we are. The cycle continues. We do "it" again.

> *As a dog returns to its vomit, so a fool repeats his folly.*

> **—Proverbs 26:11**

What is "it" for you?

Having a temper with your family? Overspending out of greed? Gluttony? Drinking beyond moderation? Imagining what life would have been like if you had married *him*? Talking behind your friends' back again? Pornography?

What is "it" for you?

Some people don't change because they don't even know what "it" is anymore. "It's just who I am..." says the negative, critical person. "God made me this way." God made you to sin? I don't think so. God made you to reflect Him. God doesn't sin. God is holy. And He is calling you to become like Him. So own up to "it". Call "it" by it's worst name. Call "it" sin. Call "it" vomit.

We need to travel BACKWARDS to examine our experiences with "it." When does "it" happen? Why did we do "it" again?

Were you tired? Are you neglecting time with Jesus in prayer and reflection? Do you need to meet with a counselor? Do you have guilt built up inside? Are you alone?

What "same things" are you doing over and over that lead you to "it"?

Examine your life. Examine your experiences. Change your routine. Don't be insane anymore: don't be alone online, don't go to that party, don't talk about finances when you haven't slept well, don't take your credit card in your wallet, don't Facebook your ex-boyfriend...

Don't do the same thing over and over again.

Examine your life. Change your routine.

"It" won't disappear overnight. But "it" will lose power over your life as *you* change your pathways and choose a routine that brings you towards Jesus instead.

ACTION:

Find out what "it" is. Maybe there are several. Write your sin(s) out on a piece of paper. Next to "it", write what leads to "it", why you do "it" and when "it" happens. Pray. Confess your sin to Jesus and ask Him to lead you away from the circumstances that lead to your sin. Consider talking with a friend or your spouse. If "it" is really entrenched in your life, get into a recovery program or see a counselor. Deal with "it."

MY THOUGHTS / PLAN OF ACTION

_____
_____
_____
_____
_____
_____
_____
_____
_____
_____
_____

TODAY'S DATE

_____

GROW BACKWARDS   day FIVE

FOR A PURPOSE...

The discipline of examination is not just a mental exercise. Growing backwards grows our soul to become like Jesus. And it has to lead to action.

In high school, we spent hours working on trigonometry. We were taught all the different math symbols. We measured lines. We discovered angles. We memorized formulas. Five days a week, we had math for one hour at 8:00 am. Five days a week, we had homework filled with problems and mental strain. Each quarter, we had an extensive math exam covering three months of learning. This final examination took hours of preparation.

At home, I would look through the math book, I would talk through the problems with a friend, we would look through completed homework, and occasionally, I would ask my parents for help.

My dad would look at the problems, make some points, and tell me to talk to my mom. My mom would glance at the study guide and refer me to my dad. This always amazed me. How could my parents have forgotten? They too had completed trigonometry. They had spent hours studying and completing exams... now they forgot?

More than a decade has gone by since those long days of diligent study. I barely remember any of my learning. All of those graded papers mean nothing to me now. Where did all of that knowledge go?

We forget so much of the knowledge we learn.

Why?

We don't keep practicing it. We have no use for it. It doesn't serve a purpose now.

A friend of mine is in the midst of studying mathematics. For him it is not just a mental exercise, it's pragmatic. For him, it is helpful; it is his future field of employment. He wants to become an engineer. He immerses himself in math, and he will remember it because it serves a purpose.

The follower of Jesus engages in self-examination with a purpose. The Christian travels BACKWARDS in order to travel towards Christ.

Take your journal, take your poetry, take your confession, take your remembering and do something with it. Let it instruct you in the future. Let it lead you to praising God. Let it teach you, inform you, guide you, help you… Let your past and your ponderings reveal what needs to be done in the present…

The Hebrew prophet Ezekiel chided Israel for not remembering the lessons they had learned from their past (**Ezekiel 16:43**). They had stopped examining their ways and had come to live wicked lives, which ignored their Creator and God.

Was it simply remembering and examining that Ezekiel wanted them to do? Was it simply a mental exercise that Ezekial asked of them? No. He was calling them to travel BACKWARDS so that they could grow *towards* their God.

> *... Then you will remember your ways and be ashamed... I will establish my covenant with you, and you will know that I am the LORD. Then, when I make atonement for you for all you have done...*
>
> **—Ezekiel 16:61-63**

There is more to this passage. But even a simple reading warns you and me not to forget where we have been, or to neglect the condition of our interior.

There may be no danger in passing up trigonometry and letting it go unpracticed. But there is great danger to our soul in passing up the discipline of examination and not practicing the actions it leads us to.

So what does the discipline of examination do to you? Do you need to go back and ask forgiveness from a friend? Do you need to wrestle through some tension and enter some discussions? Do you need to remember the great things God has done, then praise Him?

Do you need to do acts of restitution?

Do you need to pray prayers of repentance?

Do you need to engage in works of restoration?

Examine yourself.

Do it on purpose.

Then act on it.

MEMORIZE

Do not merely listen to the word, and so deceive yourselves. Do what it says.—
James 1:22 (NIV)

MY THOUGHTS / PLAN OF ACTION

_____

_____

_____

_____

_____

_____

_____

_____

_____

TODAY'S DATE

_____

day FIVE:
GROW BACKWARDS

week TWO: GROW FORWARDS

Moving forward is acting out the commission that Jesus gave to all his followers, 'go and make disciples.' GROWING FORWARDS is the discipline of **witness**. It is knowing your redemption story and telling it to others. It is inviting others to find their own story with Jesus so that the redemption movement grows and extends to all nations and all people.

GROW FORWARDS day ONE

SHOW & TELL

"Class, tomorrow is show and tell…"

Say those words to a room full of kindergartners and what will you get? Murmurs of excitement, creative ideas floating through their minds, fidgety kids shaken with anticipation. They simply cannot contain themselves. Kids cannot wait to show off their treasures to the world.

Throughout life, our excitement to show off our treasure remains. Sometimes, it hides under the surface, but it is still there. If you ask to see kid's pictures from a mom, she will take you straight to her collection. If you ask a musician to tell you about their craft, even someone shy will be able to extol their passion. If you talk to a motor-head, get ready; he will know the size, specifications, manufacturing dates… enough to fill up a manual. It's not just kids; people of all ages enjoy showing off their treasures.

Why is it then that many Christians tend to not get so excited in talking about Jesus?

After all, we sing songs about how God is our treasure. There are parables, which compare the Kingdom of God to some great treasure. Pastors preach sermons reminding us of how great a treasure the gospel is. So why don't we get excited about showing others and telling others about this treasure?

This isn't to guilt you. This is to remind **us**. Even a kindergartner won't show the same treasure day after day. The kids get used to their toys, then they move on to a new favorite. As kids get used to their toys, we (Christians) can get used to God's life. What once was so valuable to us now stays on the shelf of our mind to be enjoyed once or twice a week amongst other Christians. Now we don't go, show and tell the world who Jesus sends us to; instead we share and pray with those who are already enjoying the treasure just like we do.

Do you see yourself in this description? I hope not. I hope that you are so excited about what God has done for you:

- Saved you from the consequence of your sin...
- Given you hope of everlasting life...
- Rescued you from the power of death...
- Freed you from the devil's hold...
- Redeemed your purpose on earth...
- Blessed you with everything you have...
- Granted you the keys to life through the Bible...
- Put His Holy Spirit in you...
- Shown you a better way to live...

... And the list goes on. I hope that you are so excited about what God has done for you that you act like a kindergartner at Show & Tell. I pray that you bubble over with excitement and anticipation to show others that way of life Jesus has called his followers to. I pray that you squirm with delight at the idea of telling your friends, acquaintances and family about God's great treasure.

Be assured of this: the message of Jesus is the greatest treasure ever! Paul marveled in his letter to the Roman church about the nature of this message:

> ... *And that message is the very message about faith that we preach: If you confess with your mouth that Jesus is Lord and believe in your heart that God raised him from the dead, you will be saved. For it is by believing in your heart that you are made right with God, and it is by confessing with your mouth that you are saved... "Everyone who calls on the name of the Lord will be saved."*

—Romans 10:8-10,13

The treasure is meant for "Everyone". It's meant to be seen and heard. But there is a problem. Paul goes on to tell us:

> *But how can they call on him to save them unless they believe in him? And how can they believe in him if they have never heard about him? And how can they hear about him unless someone tells them? And how will anyone go and tell them without being sent? That is why the Scriptures say, "How beautiful are the feet of messengers who bring good news!"*

—Romans 10:14-15

What's the problem? It's not that people don't want the treasure. It's not that people aren't ready to hear about Jesus. It's not that there aren't enough Christians. The problem is that people are not going. Jesus' followers aren't Showing and Telling.

It's time to reawaken your excitement. It's time to put God's life on display in your life. It's time to tell your friends about what God has done for you. This is your mission. This is your reminder. This is your direction.

You are sent out on God's mission.

REFLECT ON JESUS' COMMISSION:

Jesus came and told his disciples, "I have been given all authority in heaven and on earth. Therefore, go and make disciples of all the nations, baptizing them in the name of the Father and the Son and the Holy Spirit. Teach these new disciples to obey all the commands I have given you. And be sure of this: I am with you always, even to the end of the age."—**Matthew 28:19-20**

As he spoke, he showed them the wounds in his hands and his side. They were filled with joy when they saw the Lord! Again he said, "Peace be with you. As the Father has sent me, so I am sending you." Then he breathed on them and said, "Receive the Holy Spirit. If you forgive anyone's sins, they are forgiven. If you do not forgive them, they are not forgiven."—**John 20:20b-23**

MY THOUGHTS / PLAN OF ACTION

_____
_____
_____
_____
_____
_____
_____
_____
_____
_____
_____
_____

TODAY'S DATE

_____

GROW FORWARDS   day TWO

INCREDIBLE VISTAS

These are some of my favorites views.

Driving down the roads of Washington State on a crisp fall day. The road is lined with multi-hued trees. Orange, yellow, red, brown, green leaves hug the branches. One by one, they let go and flitter to the ground. It's beautiful.

Sitting on the beach at Marblehead, Massachusetts. The Atlantic Ocean stretches on before the eyes. The water is frigid but the sunrays are warm and entice you to take a nap on the chilly sand. It's peaceful.

Hiking at Rancho Las Moras outside of Mazatlan, Mexico. The desert hills roll on to create a mountainous wilderness. Cacti litter the dry shell of the earth. Snakes, wild critters and peacocks(!) cross your path. The land is barren and it's full of life? How does that work? It's amazing.

Flying over farmlands. Skiing between the mountains. Taking pictures at sunset. Running through the forest. Walking through a field of wheat. Slowing the car through the South Dakota badlands. Basking in the tropical sun.

I could go on. But what about you? What are some of your favorite views of earth? Do you prefer the spring when flowers begin to bloom? Do you enjoy the long days of summer and staying up to see the sunset? Or do you like to travel to well known places such as the Grand Canyon? Think about it for a moment. Close your eyes and picture an incredible vista you have witnessed.

(SERIOUSLY. DO IT.)

The famous Israelite King, David, started out as a wandering shepherd. He walked through countless landscapes. He had witnessed spectacular sky shows. He regularly gauged the weather forecast by taking in his environmental surroundings. He *knew* the beauty of the earth.

After experiencing and appreciating many of the wonders of God's creation, David came to a conclusion:

> *The heavens proclaim the glory of God.*
> *The skies display his craftsmanship.*
> *Day after day they continue to speak;*
> *night after night they make him known.*
> *They speak without a sound or word;*
> *their voice is never heard.*
> *Yet their message has gone throughout the earth,*
> *and their words to all the world.*

—Psalm 19:1-4

David seemed to think that the earth itself has a message to share. The beauties, the wonders, the views of earth proclaim, display and speak of God. Night after night, creation points people to the God who created it.

The earth is a witness to God.

The Apostle Paul agreed with David. He wrote in his letter to the Romans:

> *(People) know the truth about God because he has made it obvious to them. For ever since the world was created, people have seen the earth and sky. Through everything God made,*

> *they can clearly see his invisible qualities—his eternal power and divine nature. So they have no excuse for not knowing God.*

—Romans 1:19-20

So, all of God's creation recognizes and praises God…

… except for one group: People.

Paul continues his train of thought:

> *Yes, they knew God, but they wouldn't worship him as God or even give him thanks. And they began to think up foolish ideas of what God was like. As a result, their minds became dark and confused. Claiming to be wise, they instead became utter fools. And instead of worshiping the glorious, ever-living God, they worshiped idols made to look like mere people and birds and animals and reptiles.*

—Romans 1:21-23

Some people flat out refuse to acknowledge God, and so they don't praise Him. They don't believe in God, so they follow their own desires.

My guess is that this doesn't describe you since you are reading this book about becoming like God. That's probably not a problem you relate with. Just because you acknowledge God, though, doesn't mean you are GROWING FORWARDS; just because you believe in God doesn't mean you are a witness to God.

So let me ask you. Are you doing your part?

Do you proclaim the glory of God?

Do you display God's craftsmanship?

Do you speak about Jesus, God in flesh, and make Him known?

If not, then you are among the only creation that does not. The skies, the animals, the landscapes, the oceans, the mountains are all making God known. Even the silent universe is speaking God's name. Isn't it fitting that we would do the same?

David ended his psalm with a prayer:

> *May the words of my mouth*
> *and the meditation of my heart*
> *be pleasing to you,*
> *O LORD, my rock and my redeemer.*

—Psalm 19:14

David didn't want to miss out on His role in making God known to others. David didn't want to be the only part of creation that didn't recognized and give honor to the Creator. David wanted to do his part and he did.

David wrote poems and songs that point to God. Millions of people have read these writings.

- David told King Saul and the Israelite army that God was a powerful God and could help them (**1 Samuel 17**).
- David organized worship celebrations for the people when he was King (**2 Samuel 6**).

- David chastised his wife Michal when she disdained his worship of God (**2 Samuel 6**).
- David gathered money and material to build a massive temple to God that foreigners traveled to come see (**2 Samuel 7**).

David spoke about God. David lived a life of worship to God. David wrote about God. David witnessed to the glory, power and reality of God.

What if you and I did the same? It's time to GROW FORWARD. It's time to commit to becoming verbal witnesses of God. It's time to pray:

May the words of my mouth
 and the meditation of my heart
be pleasing to you,
 O LORD, my rock and my redeemer.

ACTION:

Who are some people around you to whom you can tell your God story? Invite them out to coffee or to your home or to lunch after a church gathering; afterwards, tell them how it is that you came to put your faith in Jesus. Tell them why you choose to follow God.

MY THOUGHTS / PLAN OF ACTION

_____
_____
_____
_____
_____
_____
_____
_____
_____
_____
_____

TODAY'S DATE

_____

GROW FORWARDS day THREE

INVESTMENTS & ARROWS

There are many ways to invest your money. When I was 19 years old, I chose a mutual fund. Each month I put a mere $50.00 into my fund. Each week I looked through the newspaper, found my fund and watched to see what happened with my investment. Did it go up? Did it stand still? Did it drop?

I didn't know much about mutual funds or stocks, but I did know that I cared about what happened with my money. And since I cared about my money, I cared about my fund.

We care about what we are invested in.

On Sundays, I go to our church gathering and I do my part. I serve. I welcome guests. I pray. I sing. I give. I do my part, and I typically care about what happens.

Then... there are Sundays... those special Sundays... when someone I invited from the soccer team that I coach comes... or when a family member I pray for regularly comes... or when a neighbor or friend shows up at church... on *those* days... I *really* care about what happens: I pray that the preaching is *incredible*. I want everyone from the church to be *extra* welcoming. I hope the music is *phenomenal*.

When I invite my friends to church, my investment in a Sunday gathering increases. Inviting my friends to church increases my level of care and intensity of prayer.

When we invite people to church, when we share our Jesus story, when we tell people that we follow Jesus, our faith begins to means more. *Now* we have something on the line. *Now* we know someone is watching us. *Now* we realize that what we say and how we act really matters. *Now* the arrows of our heart turn outwards. We care for others. We pray for others. We love others.

What happens when you have nothing invested in your church? What happens when no one knows that you are follower of Jesus? What happens when you don't feel the need to be a witness to Jesus? The arrows of your heart turn inwards. Since you aren't invested in God's mission, all you care about is your own comfort.

Jesus always had the arrows of His heart turned outwards. Jesus was immensely invested in people coming to know Him as their God and savior. As Jesus walked the earth, He noticed people that others didn't because Jesus had invested His life. Here's one example:

> *As Jesus was walking along, he* **saw** *a man named Matthew sitting at his tax collector's booth. "Follow me and be my disciple," Jesus* **said** *to him. So Matthew got up and followed him.*
>
> **—Matthew 9:9** *(emphasis added)*

Jesus invited this unloved individual to follow Him. No one else noticed the potential of Matthew. Jesus did.

Jesus called Matthew to follow Him. Matthew threw a party.

> *Later, Matthew **invited** Jesus and his disciples to his home as dinner guests, **along with many** tax collectors and other disreputable sinners.*
>
> —**Matthew 9:10** *(emphasis added)*

Matthew realized what Jesus was doing for him. Matthew realized the grace that God was giving him. Matthew understood that Jesus was including him. So what does Matthew do? He imitates Jesus, thinking, 'if Jesus is inviting me, I should invite others.'

It makes sense. Jesus has His arrows turned out. Jesus is on mission. Jesus is pointing people to a relationship with God the Father. It makes sense that His followers would do the same.

Imagine that dinner setting. They are all gathering together for a meal: Jesus comes with some of his followers (along with some religious insiders—the Pharisees). Matthew is present with some of his sinful friends whom he invites because he wants them to meet Jesus. What do you think Matthew felt like? Do you think he was nervous that his friends wouldn't get included amongst the insiders? Do you think that he was worried about what people would think of them? Do you think he was trying extra hard to introduce these friends to Jesus?

I think so.

Matthew was invested. So the arrows of his heart and attention turned outwards.

Here's what happens when you aren't invested:

> *But when the Pharisees saw this, they asked his disciples, "Why does your teacher eat with such scum?"*

> **—Matthew 9:11**

The Pharisees were the religious insiders. They took God's grace for granted. They weren't on mission. They didn't feel the need to be a witness to God's love. They didn't have time, money or effort invested in inviting people to meet God. What happened to their hearts? The arrows turned inwards.

> *When Jesus heard this, he said, "Healthy people don't need a doctor—sick people do." Then he added, "Now go and learn the meaning of this Scripture: 'I want you to show mercy, not offer sacrifices.' For I have come to call not those who think they are righteous, but those who know they are sinners."*

> **—Matthew 9:12-13**

Jesus is very clear about His mission. He came to call those who know they are sinners. Jesus came for people who are outside of relationship with God. Jesus came with arrows out. He asks His followers to do the same.

What direction are your arrows? When was the last time you went out of the way to display God's love and grace to people outside of the religious circle? When was the last time you purposefully invited someone to your church?

Maybe you do this each week. I hope so. I pray that this is the case. It's a far more exciting way to live the Christian life. Like a 19-year-old who anxiously watches his fifty-dollar investment, you will find yourself caring a lot more about what happens.

As you invest yourself, you will ask your friends to be inclusive, you will pray that the Pastor preaches well, you will ask God to help you live a holier life and you will pray for opportunities to share your God story.

As you invest more in God's mission, the arrows of your heart will turn further and further out. In doing so, your heart will become more and more like the heart of Jesus.

REFLECTION:

People are inviting their friends and loved ones to your church. They are hoping that you will be like Jesus to their friends instead of like a Pharisee. Next time you see someone whom you don't recognize in your church gathering, turn your arrows outwards, get away from your friends and make the gathering extra special to those who have been invited.

MY THOUGHTS / PLAN OF ACTION

_____
_____
_____
_____
_____
_____
_____
_____
_____
_____
_____

TODAY'S DATE

_____

GROW FORWARDS   day **FOUR**

BEING SAVED

I was out with three new friends and we started talking about faith, God, religion, the Bible and my own journey of becoming a Christian. As we talked, I somehow ended up using the word, "saved". The conversation stopped. One friend looked at me and asked, "What does that mean?" He didn't know. I paused. I was new to living out this journey of faith. I knew in my heart what I meant, but I wasn't sure how to explain it. I stumbled a bit in my answer. He jumped on my hesitation and expressed his frustration with what he called religion. "Saved from what? *Why* do I need to be saved? I like my life. I don't need to be saved. I'm perfectly fine the way I am."

Our conversation was going great until I used a loaded word, and my friend wasn't sure what it was loaded with. To be fair, I wasn't sure what it was loaded with either. "Saved" and other words that religious insiders use and which frequent popular translations of the Bible are sometimes referred to as 'christianese.'

chris·tian·ese [kris-chuh-eez]—noun

1. the language that religious insiders speak to each other while those on the outside have no idea what they are saying.

2. catchphrases used by some Christians influenced by popular Bible translations, theology and religious media.

Words such as "saved", "lamb of God", "born again", "blessed", and others are great words with deep significance. Yet, for someone who has not grown up around the Bible or has not been part of a church, these words can be confusing. While talking with my friends that day, I should have told them *my* story. I should have told them how I realized I had a new mission in life. I should have explained to them the hope that I have. I could have shared with them that I had peace. There were many ways to tell my story and how God has helped me, changed me and redirected me. But I got caught using christianese and my friend sidetracked me from telling my God story into trying to explain theology that I didn't quite understand yet.

Understanding what being saved means is important:

> *Once you were dead because of your disobedience and your many sins. You used to live in sin, just like the rest of the world, obeying the devil—the commander of the powers in the unseen world. He is the spirit at work in the hearts of those who refuse to obey God. All of us used to live that way, following the passionate desires and inclinations of our sinful nature. By our very nature we were subject to God's anger, just like everyone else.*
>
> *But God is so rich in mercy, and he loved us so much, that even though we were dead because of our sins, he gave us life when he raised Christ from the dead. (It is only by God's grace that you have been **saved**!) For he raised us from the dead along with*

Christ and seated us with him in the heavenly realms because we are united with Christ Jesus. So God can point to us in all future ages as examples of the incredible wealth of his grace and kindness toward us, as shown in all he has done for us who are united with Christ Jesus.

*God **saved** you by his grace when you believed. And you can't take credit for this; it is a gift from God. Salvation is not a reward for the good things we have done, so none of us can boast about it.*

—**Ephesians 2:1-9** *(emphasis added)*

This passage is of incredible importance to the follower of Jesus. It explains what God has rescued us from. It reveals God's mercy. It points out *why* we need to be saved.

But it doesn't stop there.

Don't stop at *why* you were saved. Don't stop at being thankful for God's grace. Don't stop at understanding what God has done for you. Don't stop at being able to explain salvation. Don't stop there.

Don't stop at the *why*. Continue on to explore the *what for*.

What were we saved for? For what purpose has God given us new life? What is God's grace given to us for?

For we are God's masterpiece. He has created us anew in Christ Jesus, so we can do the good things he planned for us long ago.

—Ephesians 2:10

God redeemed us (restored value to us). God saved us (rescued us from our sin and its consequence). God gave us grace (we don't deserve anything from God). God did all this so that *we* can go and "do the good things he planned for us". What does that entail? God has saved you so that you can bring His salvation to others.

So go learn theology. Then go live it out in such a way that your friends can understand that they too have a need for God.

REFLECTION:

What do you think about Ephesians 2:10? How does this make you feel?

MY THOUGHTS / PLAN OF ACTION

_____

_____

_____

_____

_____

_____

_____

_____

_____

_____

_____

TODAY'S DATE

_____

GROW FORWARDS   day FIVE

FOCUS ON WHAT YOU KNOW

Some people are amazing with cars. They can fix anything. I am not one of them.

Occasionally, my car acts up: the emergency brake no longer holds my car in place, the engine jumps up and hits the hood, the steering wheel won't turn... those are real problems I've had without any idea how to fix them. Each time I take my car down to the same place to get it fixed. Each time the mechanic analyzes the problem, gives me the estimate and then gets to work.

Time passes. My car is fixed. I go on with driving.

Occasionally a friends' car acts up too. They tell me their symptoms. I nod my head. Not because I understand what the problem is and how to fix it, but because I feel their pain. It is then that I point my friend to my mechanic. We take their car down to the same place I go to get my car fixed. The mechanic figures out the problem and gives them the solution.

I don't understand how my car is fixed. I don't understand how my friends' cars are fixed. I just know who can fix it.

You may be reading this week's discipline of witness with a fear that you don't know enough: You don't think you know what to say to people about Jesus. You don't know how to explain who God is. You feel inadequate with theology. You worry about what will happen when someone asks you a tricky question.

STOP: Just focus on what you know.

In the **Gospel of John, chapter 10**, we read about a beggar who meets Jesus. This man has been blind all his life. Jesus prays for him. The blind man receives sight. Needless to say, this man has a story. He still doesn't know much though. All he knows is that Jesus has healed his eyes.

The beggar's neighbors see him walking around without his cane. They notice the change in this man. It's obvious. In fact, the change is so big they wonder if the beggar is really the man who once was blind. In a humorous dialogue the beggar essentially says, "Hey, LOOK! It really is me." To which they reply, "How did this happen?" "Ummmmm... Jesus healed me. That's all I know."

This blind beggar meets Jesus. Jesus changes his life. He doesn't understand theology. He does not even realize that Jesus is God in flesh. All he knows is that Jesus healed him.

Don't wait until you have more information, knowledge and experience. Simply start telling people about what you do know:

> "I used to worry about what would happen after death, but now I don't. I met Jesus."

> "All my life I have tried so hard to get people to accept me and now I *feel* accepted by God. I met Jesus."

"There are so many regrets I have from being in the gang. I did things that I feel really bad about. But I know Jesus has forgiven me, and now I want to help others. Why? I met Jesus."

These quotes are the essence of real life conversations that I have had with people who have met Jesus. One was a teenager. One was a successful entrepreneur. One was fresh out of a gang. None of them knew theology at the time. The former gang member is now reading his Bible. The business lady is starting to read some theology along with her new Bible. The teenager grew up and went through Bible schooling.

They are growing in their understanding, but at first it was simply, "I met Jesus and my life has changed."

Go back to John, chapter 10. After talking with his neighbors, the formerly blind man encounters a group of people who want nothing to do with Jesus. They don't think Jesus healed the man. They don't want to follow Jesus. They don't want this man to follow Jesus, and so they try to disprove Jesus.

As you read this story, notice a couple of details:

1. See what he says when he doesn't know an answer. (One of his statements isn't actually true: God does listen to sinners. He doesn't know theology but he stays in the conversation.)

2. Look at the boldness of the healed man. He knows *his* story and he's sticking to it.

3. Consider how eager he is at the end to find out more about Jesus. Then notice how he starts worshipping Jesus as God.

So for the second time they called in the man who had been blind and told him, "God should get the glory for this, because we know this man Jesus is a sinner."

"I don't know whether he is a sinner," the man replied. "But I know this: I was blind, and now I can see!"

"But what did he do?" they asked. "How did he heal you?"

"Look!" the man exclaimed. "I told you once. Didn't you listen? Why do you want to hear it again? Do you want to become his disciples, too?"

Then they cursed him and said, "You are his disciple, but we are disciples of Moses! We know God spoke to Moses, but we don't even know where this man comes from."

"Why, that's very strange!" the man replied. "He healed my eyes, and yet you don't know where he comes from? We know that God doesn't listen to sinners, but he is ready to hear those who worship him and do his will. Ever since the world began, no one has been able to open the eyes of someone born blind. If this man were not from God, he couldn't have done it."

"You were born a total sinner!" they answered. "Are you trying to teach us?" And they threw him out of the synagogue.

When Jesus heard what had happened, he found the man and asked, "Do you believe in the Son of Man?"

The man answered, "Who is he, sir? I want to believe in him."

"You have seen him," Jesus said, "and he is speaking to you!"

"Yes, Lord, I believe!" the man said. And he worshiped Jesus.

—John 10:24-38

I don't know how to personally fix my car, but that doesn't stop me from getting it fixed. It doesn't stop me from helping others.

You might not understand the whole Gospel message, you might not personally understand theology, but that didn't stop you from meeting Jesus. It doesn't stop you from helping others meet Jesus either.

Should you learn about what God has done for you? Absolutely. Should you take a class on theology? That's a great idea.

Should you read the Bible and get to know the Gospel? Yes!

Just don't let your lack of understanding keep you from telling others about what Jesus has done in you. When you are asked questions you don't have an answer for, tell them you don't know. Do some research, then come back and give the answer.

Don't be afraid of what you don't know.

Just focus on what you know and tell people: "I met Jesus and you can know Him too."

PRAY & TELL:

Who are five people that you are praying for to meet Jesus? Pray for them and then look for opportunities to tell them your story.

1. _____
2. _____
3. _____
4. _____
5. _____

MY THOUGHTS / PLAN OF ACTION

_____
_____
_____
_____
_____
_____
_____
_____
_____
_____
_____
_____

TODAY'S DATE

_____

week THREE: GROW WITHWARDS

What does 'withwards' mean? It is the idea that no one does life alone. No one goes at it alone. Nobody does the mission of God alone. Life is best traveled together. Here's the problem–Sin. Sin separates. Sin tears us apart. Sin divides. So how can we be GROWING WITHWARDS? This takes us to the discipline of regular **confession** and spoken **forgiveness**…

GROW WITHWARDS   day ONE

BARE NAKED

Ah, counseling…

One day a foreign thought presented itself to my mind: "I should go see a counselor."

What! Go see a counselor? Why? I've never been abused. I haven't experienced divorce. I've grieved the loss of loved ones in a healthy manner. I had a good childhood. There were no reasons for me to go see a counselor. I ignored this thought in my head and continued on with life.

One evening, after a great day with work and friends, I was sitting in my newly purchased condo and something broke inside of me. I wept. Tears streamed down my face and I had no idea why. I was confused. I was embarrassed. I was shocked. What was wrong with me?

Two months later, I sat across from a counselor. She asked me why I had come to see her. *Why had I come to see her?* I didn't really know. I just started talking and talking and talking. She asked questions and took me even deeper. At the end of two hours, I was in tears talking about matters of doubt, insecurity, fear, regret and love.

It was like my soul was laid bare-naked.

I felt great. Amidst streaming hot tears, I felt more like myself than I had for a long, long, long time.

Over the next several months, I met with this counselor. We uncovered angst, sin, struggles and anger. Sometimes, I laughed. Sometimes, I went away energized. Sometimes, I cried. Sometimes, I hid my face. Conversation by conversation, the masks of dirty dust that hid my soul were removed. I was becoming more and more free. My soul was living with less and less covering...

God created you to live with a bare-naked soul.

> *So the LORD God caused the man to fall into a deep sleep. While the man slept, the LORD God took out one of the man's ribs and closed up the opening. Then the LORD God made a woman from the rib, and he brought her to the man.*
>
> *"At last!" the man exclaimed.*
> *"This one is bone from my bone,*
> *and flesh from my flesh!*
> *She will be called 'woman,'*
> *because she was taken from 'man.'"*

—Genesis 2:21-25

This explains why a man leaves his father and mother and is joined to his wife, and the two are united into one.

Now the man and his wife were both naked, but they felt no shame.

Sin came into the perfect picture and marred mankind.

Since then, sin has continued to sink our soul under layers of coverings. When we are sinned against and hurt, we cover our soul with a myriad of responses: fake smiles, manipulation, withdrawal, sarcasm, stonewalling, and many more. When we sin against others, we also cover up our soul with regret, hardheartedness, pride, rejection…

We sin. We are sinned against. Our soul bears the burden.

But there is hope. Jesus offers a way out:

> *"Come to me, all of you who are weary and carry heavy burdens, and I will give you rest."*
>
> **—Matthew 11:28**

I sat in the chair face to face with a counselor. There were only two visible faces, but three people were present. God was with us. When I confessed to her, He took my burden. Through our natural conversation, God was supernaturally involved.

Both are needed.

See, maybe you feel like you don't need a counselor. You probably don't (even though it wouldn't hurt anything but your bank account). Maybe you think you can just go to God and confess your sins. After all, it is true. You can just go to God. But if that's all you ever do, there may be some sins that *you* won't be able to let go of without sitting face to face with a friend.

Or, maybe you feel like you don't need to confess your sins to God. You have bought into our modern reliance on human counselors. After all, by talking through your issues with someone, won't they go away? But if that's all you ever do, you will never deal with the root problem of the sin that led to your issues.

Both are needed. You need someone to listen and you must have God to carry your burden away.

Many souls are cluttered by dusty long overlooked sins. The sin has never been dealt with. They are wounds that fester. They are hurts that grow. They are problems that become entrenched. They are chains that hold you back from being free. It's time to verbalize your sin to another. It's time to have the courage to sit face to face with a friend or a friendly counselor. It's time to confess to God in the presence of another. It's time to live free, uncluttered and forgiven. It's time to bare your soul.

QUESTIONS:

Who do you confess your recurring sins to?
Are there issues that you haven't dealt with?
Do you need to see a counselor or pastor?
Is you soul cluttered or is it naked?

MY THOUGHTS / PLAN OF ACTION

_____

_____

_____

_____

_____

_____

_____

_____

_____

_____

TODAY'S DATE

_____

day ONE:
GROW WITHWARDS

GROW WITHWARDS   day **TWO**

RAISING CAIN

Siblings can be annoying.

Growing up there is no one better and no one worse to fight with than your brother or sister. There is no one better, because most likely they will forgive you, and most often they are nearby in case you are feeling contentious. There is no one worse, because an unforgiving sibling will haunt you through life, and since they are family, there is no getting away.

Siblings. Some have many. Some have few. What's the point of having any? Companionship–someone to be with growing up and throughout life. Acceptance–my older sister knows my flaws and has since the beginning; yet she still loves me. Fun– there is so much insider language with a sibling, so many memories and you get to enjoy that all of your life. Growth...

One of the reasons that God has given us siblings is so that we can grow up to be the people He created us to be. Think about it from two perspectives: negatively and positively.

NEGATIVELY:

Brothers and sisters can be so annoying. Brothers can be so cruel. Sisters can be so mean. They can hurt you. They can make you feel inferior. They can push your buttons. They can push your buttons. Your siblings *know* how to bring out the worst in you.

And you have a choice of how to respond.

The first brothers in God's creation were Cain and Abel. Both brothers gave gifts or offerings to God. Abel's offering was accepted. Cain's offering was not. Cain was furious. He was jealous of his brother. He was embittered towards his brother. He was frustrated with his brother. He felt threatened by his younger brother. And so…

> *"One day Cain suggested to his brother, 'Let's go out into the fields.' And while they were in the field, Cain attacked his brother, Abel, and killed him."*

—Genesis 4:8

Cain murdered his brother. My guess is that you have never done that. Perhaps you have wanted to! Maybe you have wished it… but you have never done it. Or have you? Jesus taught us that hatred towards a brother is murder in the heart. My guess is that at some point *you* have come close to murder in your heart.

It's usually not without reason either. I can easily imagine the younger brother Abel taunting the older brother Cain. Can't you? When a younger siblings get the upper hand, how do they respond? They use it to annoy and irritate the older siblings. This leads to frustration, irritation, anger, and if it keeps on growing… hate.

God gave us siblings so that we can grow to become the holy people He made us to be. In every negative situation, you *can* respond positively. With every positive, loving, gracious, faithful, kind, helpful and forgiving response your soul grows since you imitate the very way of life that God initiates.

Every time we look to Jesus and forgive the sin of our 'brothers' and 'sisters'… every time we choose to respond with love instead of hate… every time we slow down and choose to encourage instead of cursing our siblings…

… every time we choose forgiveness we grow. We have overcome evil with God's goodness.

POSITIVELY:

I'd prefer never to be confronted with the evil workings of negative relationships. And God never intended for evil to be in our relationships. He desired that we grow with our fellow men and women from a positive perspective.

> *"Afterward the* LORD *asked Cain, 'Where is your brother? Where is Abel?'*
>
> *'I don't know,' Cain responded. 'Am I my brother's guardian?'*
>
> *But the* LORD *said, 'What have you done? Listen! Your brother's blood cries out to me from the ground!'"*
>
> **—Genesis 4:9-11**

Cain essentially answered God, 'Am I my brother's guardian? Am I his keeper? Am I his confidante, comforter and companion? Do I have to walk through life and help my brother? Am I supposed to only do what is good to him? Am I supposed to encourage him and build him up, even at my expense? Am I to be my brother's friend?'

Yes.

God created you to walk through life *with* your family. You are to encourage them. Treat them with respect. Give them love. Build them up. Help them out. Give your life to them. Support them. You are to guard their life, not drain them of life.

You don't grow alone. You grow in family, both your home family and your church family. You don't travel life alone. Your faith in God and your journey with Jesus is not only personal, it's familial. So who are you traveling with?

Who are you encouraging, supporting, helping out and serving?

Who do you need to forgive, have patience with and pray for?

This matters. You have to travel this life *with* others. You need to make matters right *with* those around you. This is serious. Cain took it lightly and it cost him heavily…

THINK ABOUT IT:

"Now you are cursed and banished from the ground, which has swallowed your brother's blood. No longer will the ground yield good crops for you, no matter how hard you work! From now on you will be a homeless wanderer on the earth."—
Genesis 4:11-12

MY THOUGHTS / PLAN OF ACTION

_____

_____

_____

_____

_____

_____

_____

_____

_____

TODAY'S DATE

_____

GROW WITHWARDS   day THREE

FORGIVE → BE FORGIVEN

Everyone is connected. Not physically, of course; there are millions of people you will never see. But spiritually, we are all connected. The Bible says that God is spirit. Our spirits come from His. He breathes into our bodies and our spirit comes alive. Everyone is connected back to God.

And this is how we are to journey through life. Connected.

> *"So if you are presenting a sacrifice at the altar in the Temple and you suddenly remember that someone has something against you, leave your sacrifice there at the altar. Go and be reconciled to that person. Then come and offer your sacrifice to God."*
>
> **—Matthew 5:23-24**

Ever since I was a kid, I was encouraged to have a personal relationship with God. I have one. I enjoy *my* relationship with God. I regularly pray, confess, talk to and even laugh with God as revealed in Jesus. I *personally* love Jesus, follow Jesus and imitate Jesus. It's very, very personal.

The verse you just read seems to be so much more communal and interconnected than I was ever taught. Picture this situation. Play it out in your mind.

"So if you are presenting a sacrifice... in the Temple..." Hundreds of thousands of people would travel to Jerusalem for the purpose of making a sacrifice. Jews and God-fearers would take the pilgrimage to the Temple from all over: Rome, Greece, Africa, Northern Israel (Judea)... Travel was not easy. This pilgrimage was costly, time consuming and energy draining.

"and you suddenly remember that someone has something against you..." Jesus looks out at the mass of humanity that listens to Him as He preaches. He sees the dirt-covered clothing that marks the pilgrim. He sees well-worn sandals that prove they have come a long distance. He sees the slight difference in styles that point out different lands lived in. As He sees the outside that marks their travels, He sees beyond to recognize the condition of their souls. He knows that many of them are dealing with deteriorating relationships. All of them have been sinned against and have sinned against others.

"Leave your sacrifice there at the altar." Yeah, right! Do you leave your tithing envelope out in Times Square? No. Thousands of people would frequent the Temple. Your sacrifice was a... well... it was a sacrifice. You had to give up something. Your sacrifice cost you and you wanted to give it personally to God at the Temple.

"Go and be reconciled to that person. Then come and offer your sacrifice to God." This is outrageous. Jesus is saying that your communal relationships ought to be brought to peace before you engage in personal relationship with God? Not only that, but you should leave you sacrifice, travel back to your home, make matters right with someone who has something against *you*, then travel back to Jerusalem and pick up where you left off...

What is He saying?

Jesus says, to be connected to Him is to be connected with others. Jesus says, to have a personal relationship with God is to have a communal relationship with others. This is supremely important!

I don't really like this. It does not take too much work to get on my knees and ask God to forgive me of pride, lust, or greed. It takes a lot more effort to go to someone, own up to my sin and tell them I'm sorry.

It's easier to have a personal relationship with God than to have a communal relationship with others and God. Yet, Jesus calls us to both. In fact, Jesus says to have one is to have the other. After all, we are connected.

Are you having a hard time agreeing? Read these words of Jesus:

> *"If you forgive those who sin against you, your heavenly Father will forgive you. But if you refuse to forgive others, your Father will not forgive your sins."*

—Matthew 6:14-15

Jesus says that if you and I do not forgive others then we ourselves are not forgiven! Jesus says if you and I are not connected and at peace with others, than we cannot be connected and at peace with Him.

That's tough. That's Jesus. It's true.

For a long time, I've had a personal relationship with Jesus. Now I'm learning and relearning and learning again to have a communal relationship with others. Here's what I see in my life: as I overcome sin with others, as I experience peace in my relationships with others and as I walk in openness with others, my relationship with God is more free, more peaceful, and more open. Removing the blockages and obstacles in my relationship with others has been removing hindrances in my relationships with God. Why?

Because we are all connected...

AFFIRM IT:

Add forgiveness affirmations into your daily routine. Consider waking up everyday declaring, "I am quick to forgive. I don't resent, relive grudges, or hold onto hurt. I forgive those who hurt me and I also forgive myself when I fail."

MY THOUGHTS / PLAN OF ACTION

_____
_____
_____
_____
_____
_____
_____
_____
_____

TODAY'S DATE

_____

GROW WITHWARDS day **FOUR**

A WALK ON THE LIGHTSIDE

It is not so fun to get out of bed and stumble around in darkness. It is in darkness that I stub my toe, run into tables, trip over rugs, and injure myself. I know this and yet it still keeps on happening. It is because I'm lazy. If I wake up in the middle of the night it is easier for me to shuffle in darkness to the kitchen for water than it is for me to turn on the lights. So injuries keep on happening. It is also less bothersome to walk in darkness. If I turn on the lights, it is so bright, it wakes me up, it bothers my eyes… it is just easier to walk in darkness.

A teenager wanted to talk to me after youth group one night. "Mike, I have to tell you something…" Tears came to his eyes, he looked down at the floor, he shifted his weight, and said, "Mike, I am addicted to pornography."

"How long have you been addicted?"

"Since I was twelve."

"Have you told anyone about this? Do your parents know?"

"NO!" He looked up alarmed. "You aren't going to tell them, are you?"

"No. *You* are going to tell them."

Silence.

This guy had been addicted to pornography for five years. He was racked with guilt, shame and lust. His relationships with girls were awkward. He felt disconnected from God. For five years, he did not tell anyone. He kept the light switch of his soul off. He walked in darkness, and he kept on getting hurt.

It is easier to walk in darkness, but it is not what is best.

> *But if we are living in the light, as God is in the light, then we have* **fellowship with each other***, and the blood of Jesus, his Son,* **cleanses us from all sin.**
>
> **—1 John 1:7** *(emphasis added)*

It is easier to walk in darkness, but it's fatal.

> *But if we confess our sins to him, he is faithful and just to forgive us our sins and* **to cleanse us from all wickedness.** *If we claim we have not sinned, we are calling God a liar and showing that his word* **has no place in our hearts.**
>
> **—1 John 1:9-10** *(emphasis added)*

I told the young man to tell his parents because a) they love him and want what is best for him, b) he was trying to confess his sin to me in order to avoid telling them his lengthy life of sin, c) they could actually do something to help him by taking the computer out of his room.

He never told them his sin. It was too hard because a) he didn't want to hurt them, b) direct confrontation is harder than indirect, and c) he didn't want to lose his computer privileges.

This story has repeated itself over and over again. The details, the names, and the sins are all different. But the story is the same. Teenagers make out with each other and go even further while they say that they are *studying*. Pastors log onto websites while they are supposed to be praying. Wives chat with an old boyfriend behind the backs of their husbands. Kids bully weaker kids at school while the parents think they are angels. Men ignore their families in order to stay after hours at work.

There are so many secret sins. It's shameful. It's dark. It's easy. It's fatal.

I was born a sinner. I sin. I hate it. I do not want it. I try to walk in the light. Sometimes it takes me a while to own up to my sin. Sometimes I do it right away. Light is worth it when it happens. Sometimes there are immediate consequences to confessing my sin: feelings are hurt, an argument starts or a disciplinary action is enforced. I do not like facing those consequences. No one does.

The teenager looked at me after and ended the silence.

"I can't tell my parents."

"You can't, or you won't?"

Pause. "I won't. It's too hard. I'm afraid of what will happen."

Stepping into the light may bring consequences. Living in darkness will definitely trigger fallout... eventually.

Time passed. The teenager grew distant in relationships; he fought with his parents, was harsh to his siblings and cut off some friendships (including me). The teenager distrusted God, disbelieved God, and eventually rejected God.

There is more to his story and more to my actions. But that is not for you to know. You are to know your story and what you are to do with your actions.

First: You are to walk in the light. It's worth it.

Second: You are to be someone who calls others into the light. If the teenager were to come to you... if he was your son... if he was your brother... if he was your friend... what would you have done?

Empathize and listen? "I'm so sorry..."

Many sins *are* confessed only to be dismissed. I have had loving Christians tell me at different stages of life, "It's not a big deal." sin/darkness is always a big deal. It should always be taken seriously.

Condemn and criticize? "You did what?"

Many sinners get the courage to finally confess only to be so condemned that they do not begin to walk in light, and instead they grovel in guilt.

Grace and truth. "I love you and I will help you."

An adulterous woman was brought to Jesus. He accepted her. She felt His love. He gave her grace. He told her, "I don't condemn you." He also took her sin seriously. He called her out of darkness. He called her to a new way of life, "go and sin no more."

To walk in light is to walk free from condemnation–Grace. To walk in light is to walk away from your dark tendencies–Truth.

Walking in light isn't easy. It is hard and it takes real friends who are committed to Grace and Truth. But it is always worth. So, choose the light. Turn the switch on in your life and for those around you.

ACTION:
Is there someone that you need to come alongside to help them walk in the light?

MY THOUGHTS / PLAN OF ACTION

_____
_____
_____
_____
_____
_____
_____
_____
_____
_____

TODAY'S DATE

_____

GROW WITHWARDS   day FIVE

FOREVER: STUCK OR FRIENDS

Forever is a long time.

There was a song in my youth that said, "Friends are friends *forever* if the Lord is the Lord of them."

That is a great thought isn't it? I have some incredible friends in my life that I do not get to spend a lot of time with. Some of my friends live a long ways away from me. I would love to spend more time with them. Then there are other people who haven't become friends but I really like the.

Keith came by my office and was helping me with the phone system in our church building. We interacted and laughed. He talked about his family and his work. He told me great stories and taught me the new phone system. After working on our building a couple days I could tell that I enjoyed this guy. I was going to miss him now that all his work was done. He was taking off and I wasn't going to see much of him, probably for the rest of my current earthly life.

That's what this current life looks like. Some of us might live for 80 years or even 100 years. That's not very long. In this life, we only have so many hours to invest in our family, neighbors, friends and in sharing God's story with people outside His family. We can't be friends with everyone.

Grow Your Soul

Keith lives in a different city. He has a family to take care of. He has friends he is invested in. He has a church that he serves with. He has people he is telling his God story to. And I have my life to do the same. Our lives will not intersect much...

In my office that last day, I told Keith, "I've really enjoyed getting to know you over the last couple of days and most likely we won't get to really become friends in this life, but that's okay because we have all of eternity." I meant that.

We get to spend all of eternity with people like Keith. So, I don't have to get to know him that much here. Instead, I can stay invested in my friends and I can go out on mission to those who do not know Jesus yet.

For those who have been reconciled to God through Jesus, we get to spend forever with friends and we get to make new friends forever.

> *Then, together with them, we who are still alive and remain on the earth will be caught up in the clouds to meet the Lord in the air. Then we will be with the Lord forever. So encourage each other with these words.*

—1 Thessalonians 4:17-18

Now, what about those people who belong to God's family through the work of Jesus... but who do not belong in your life? By that I mean: You-don't-like-them. What about those people? You *will* be stuck with them forever. What about those people?

"Well... I'll just deal with that later."

"There will be so many people in eternity that I can ignore those people."

"Hey, it's a big place. I'll just stay far away from them."

"It'll be different then. They won't be such a jerk."

If you are a Christian, then you are already becoming the type of person that you will be forever. The Spirit of God is already changing you, removing sin, calling you to a new way of life and making you to be like God. *Now* is the time to do what is right. We are to live at peace with all people especially with other believers because we are God's family. Postponing peace is not an option. Postponing right relationships is not an option. Postponing reconciliation is not an option.

> *Remember, it is sin to know what you ought to do and then not do it.*
>
> **—James 4:17**

> *Work at living in peace with everyone, and work at living a holy life, for those who are not holy will not see the Lord. Look after each other so that none of you fails to receive the grace of God. Watch out that no poisonous root of bitterness grows up to trouble you, corrupting many.*
>
> **—Hebrews 12:14-15**

> *Therefore, whenever we have the opportunity, we should do good to everyone—especially to those in the family of faith.*
>
> **—Galatians 6:10**

We are going to spend forever with our friends who have received the grace of Jesus. We are going to have forever to enjoy those people we like who are part of God's family. We are going to be forever with those people we do not click with, get along with, are irritated by, get frustrated by, and simply don't like.

We have a choice:

Travel away from them, ignore them, and continue to dislike them—sin.

Make the effort to journey with them, work to overcome our feelings, and pray to have God's heart towards them—grow.

Sin or Grow. It's not really a choice.

We have forever; and forever has already started. Now is the time to start GROWING WITHWARDS.

PRAYER:

Take some time right now to pray for those people who you don't mesh with or get along with. Pray that God would give you His heart for them.

MY THOUGHTS / PLAN OF ACTION

_____

_____

_____

_____

_____

_____

_____

_____

_____

_____

TODAY'S DATE

_____

week FOUR: GROW INWARDS

King David wrote that he meditated on God's words 'day and night.' God said that David was a man after His own heart. Any connection? King David was a mighty warrior; he was physically strong. But he had even greater inner strength. He filled his mind and heart with God's truth and kept coming back to God's words... GROWING INWARDS is the discipline of **meditation** & **scripture memorization**.

GROW INWARDS day **ONE**

MEDITATE-ACTIVATE

Imagine that you are the United States Speaker of the House with no ambition to become President. Then the President dies, and then the vice president dies… you are third on the chain of command. But now you are the leader of the United States…

What would you do? How would you start?

You had no ambition, no plans, no desires to lead the United States, and yet now… you are the President.

Would you pick up the Constitution and re-read it? Maybe over and over and over? Would you be counting the days until the next elections? What if the president who you took over for was the most popular and most effective president the United States had ever seen? Would you feel the pressure?

One of the great leaders of the nation of Israel was Moses. Moses and his brother Aaron performed ten great plagues to the Pharaoh of Egypt. God used Moses to part the Red Sea and free the Israelites. Moses received the famous Ten Commandments from God on Mount Sinai. Moses prayed for and received water to give drink to more than a million people in the wilderness. Moses met face to face with God. Moses talked with God. Moses led a nation for 40 years. Moses led the Israelites to defeat their enemies. Moses protected, guided, taught, encouraged, rebuked, prayed for and was responsible for an entire nation through the good times, bad times, and all the times in between.

Then Moses died.

The leadership fell to his successor–Joshua.

Joshua knew that this position of leadership would eventually be his, but I am sure it was a very daunting reality once it came to be. "How can I live up to Moses?" he must have thought. "What if I don't succeed?" he must have asked himself. "How do I assume this role of leadership?" he must have wondered.

We do not always know how to approach the future. We often do not know how to go about what God leads us to. But God knows…

> *The Book of Joshua. Chaper One.*
>
> *After the death of Moses the servant of the LORD, the LORD said to Joshua son of Nun, Moses' aide: "Moses my servant is dead. Now then, you and all these people, get ready to cross the Jordan River into the land I am about to give to them—to the Israelites. I will give you every place where you set your foot, as I promised Moses. Your territory will extend from the desert to Lebanon, and from the great river, the Euphrates—all the Hittite country—to the Mediterranean Sea in the west. No one will be able to stand against you all the days of your life. As I was with Moses, so I will be with you; I will never leave you nor forsake you. Be strong and courageous,*

because you will lead these people to inherit the land I swore to their ancestors to give them."

—**Joshua 1:1-6**

The LORD not only put Joshua in charge of His people. He also told Joshua that He would be with Joshua, just like He was with Moses. Think about how reassuring those words would be. Undoubtedly, there were times when Joshua was discouraged, frightened, doubtful... in those times he could silence his struggles, close his eyes, and come back to those words that the LORD had spoken to him, "I will be with you; I will never leave you nor forsake you..."

God chose Joshua to be the leader of Israel. And who God chooses, he also prepares.

The Story of Joshua Continued.

"Be strong and very courageous. Be careful to obey all the law my servant Moses gave you; do not turn from it to the right or to the left, that you may be successful wherever you go. Keep this Book of the Law always on your lips; meditate on it day and night, so that you may be careful to do everything written in it. Then you will be prosperous and successful. Have I not commanded you? Be strong and courageous. Do not be afraid; do not be discouraged, for the LORD your God will be with you wherever you go." So Joshua ordered

—**Joshua 1:7-10**

How did God prepare Joshua? He spoke *words* to him. God told Joshua to meditate on the *words* that He had given Moses to write. God prepared Joshua with *words* that Joshua needed to keep close to his heart. Then what happened?

"So Joshua ordered…" Joshua got to work. He started to lead.

After God gave Joshua the words of life, courage, strength, peace, and victory… after the words came the *action*. When Joshua became the leader, he didn't immediately jump into the action, he waited and meditated before he ordered and activated.

So it is with us. We start with God's words, and then we go on to Godly actions.

Meditate first. Activate after.

Slow down and be with God, so that when life speeds up, you can act Godly.

God prepared Joshua, and He will still prepare you if you will just slow down to be with Him.

ACTION:

This week it's all about meditation and memorization. Take some time to put God's words in your heart, mind and soul. Be strengthened through reading the Bible, reflecting on its words,, and memorizing some of God's promises.

Therefore, go and make disciples of all the nations, baptizing them in the name of the Father and the Son and the Holy Spirit. Teach these new disciples to obey all the commands I have given you. And be sure of this: **I am with you always***, even to the end of the age.*—**Matthew 28:19-20** *(emphasis added)*

MY THOUGHTS / PLAN OF ACTION

_____
_____
_____
_____
_____
_____
_____
_____
_____
_____

TODAY'S DATE

_____

day ONE:
GROW INWARDS

GROW INWARDS   day TWO

THE MULTIPLICATION TABLE

7 x 8 = _____

6 x 6 = _____

7 x 7 = _____

9 x 4 = _____

4 x 8 = _____

Take a moment and look at the problems up above. How fast can you answer them? Does it take some time, or is it second nature to you… 7 x 8 = 56. 6 x 6 = 36. And so on…

Mrs. Lee, my third grade teacher, made each student memorize the multiplication chart. We practiced in class, we made flash cards, we did quizzes, we exercised our memory at home and by the end of the year we were multiplication whizzes. The answers to the problems came naturally to our minds. We were ready to move on to harder math.

Several years later, I was in a new high school in a harder math class with other teenagers surrounding me. The teacher gave us algebraic equations to do. I worked the formulas, solved the problems, and gave the answers. Only a couple of the other students were ready. I was surprised. How was it taking everyone so long to work the problems? As I looked around, I noticed an odd trend: several of the high school students were working out the simple multiplication required using their hand and their margins. They were taking so long and struggling so hard because they did not have the basic truths memorized.

Multiplication: There are some things that you just need to know.

God made your mind and knows how it works. He knows the problems that come up in your life. God knows your weaknesses and He knows the power His words can have in your life to strengthen you. He knows how His instruction can help guide us in wisdom, encourage us amidst difficulty and lead us in prayer. God knows and He wants us to *know* His words.

So commit yourselves wholeheartedly to these words of mine. Tie them to your hands and wear them on your forehead as reminders.

—Deuteronomy 11:18

Over time, the Israelite people came to act this out. They committed themselves to memorizing the first five books of the Bible (many memorized much more). They created little boxes with a scripture inside to wear on their wrists and other little boxes to tie to their forehead (These were called phylacteries and orthodox Jews still wear them today). The hope of both these practices is that they would not stray from God, nor would they forget the ways of God. The hope is that you and I would not either. That is why Scripture memorization is still for today.

Memorization: There are some things that you just need to know.

MEMORIZE:

> *I tell you the truth, those who listen to my message and believe in God who sent me have eternal life. They will never be condemned for their sins, but they have already passed from death into life.*
>
> **—John 5:24**

> *And so, dear brothers and sisters, I plead with you to give your bodies to God because of all he has done for you. Let them be a living and holy sacrifice—the kind he will find acceptable. This is truly the way to worship him. Don't copy the behavior and customs of this world, but let God transform you into a new person by changing the way you think. Then you will learn to know God's will for you, which is good and pleasing and perfect.*
>
> **—Romans 12:1-2**

> *Don't worry about anything; instead, pray about everything. Tell God what you need, and thank him for all he has done. Then you will experience God's peace, which exceeds anything we can understand. His peace will guard your hearts and minds as you live in Christ Jesus.*
>
> **—Philippians 4:6-7**

Remember this—a farmer who plants only a few seeds will get a small crop. But the one who plants generously will get a generous crop. You must each decide in your heart how much to give. And don't give reluctantly or in response to pressure. "For God loves a person who gives cheerfully."

—**2 Corinthians 9:6-7**

And it is impossible to please God without faith. Anyone who wants to come to him must believe that God exists and that he rewards those who sincerely seek him.

—**Hebrews 11:6**

Trust in the LORD with all your heart;
do not depend on your own understanding.
Seek his will in all you do,
and he will show you which path to take.

—**Proverbs 3:5-6**

So let's not get tired of doing what is good. At just the right time we will reap a harvest of blessing if we don't give up. Therefore, whenever we have the opportunity, we should do good to everyone—especially to those in the family of faith.

—**Galatians 6:9-10**

In the same way, let your good deeds shine out for all to see, so that everyone will praise your heavenly Father.

—**Matthew 5:16**

NOTE:

Here are eight great passages to know and reflect on. As you do the discipline of meditation and memorization, pick up the Bible and read the whole chapter these are found in. Think about why these words were written. As you work, memorize, reflect, pray and think about how you can act these truths out.

MY THOUGHTS / PLAN OF ACTION

_____
_____
_____
_____
_____
_____
_____
_____
_____
_____
_____

TODAY'S DATE

_____

GROW INWARDS   day THREE

THE FITNESS CRAZE

How many fitness magazines exist? Hundreds? How many fitness programs have been created? Thousands? How many diet books have been written? Millions? How many times have you started to read, implement, or do something for your fitness? Countless...

These are all great things to do. I encourage you to work on your physical strength. I encourage you to take your health seriously. We should take care of our body; it is important. Paul the Apostle even acknowledges physical fitness in his letter to Timothy *"Physical training is good, but training for godliness is much better, promising benefits in this life and in the life to come."* (**1 Timothy 4:8**, *Paul is actually quoting a saying from someone else.*) So we should do physical training; it is good for us. We should build up strength, but it should not stop there. Paul tells Timothy that training in godliness is even better...

Inner strength is more important than outer strength.

Here are a couple of reasons why this is true. Here are a few reasons why we should train ourselves in godliness. Here are some reasons why we should meditate and memorize in order to grow our souls and strengthen our resolve:

OVERFLOW:

The word that we emit and the actions that we commit come from within.

> *"A good person produces good things from the treasury of a good heart, and an evil person produces evil things from the treasury of an evil heart. What you say flows from what is in your heart."*
>
> **—Luke 6:45**

Have you ever wondered why some people are more prone to hurt you with their words and actions? Inner weakness. Those people are hurting on the inside: hurt people → hurt people.

Since you want to be someone who heals people and gives life to people, *you* have to be strengthened by God on the inside. As He gives you life, heals your wounds, and grants His goodness to your heart… you will have a positive overflow to give to others.

ETERNITY:

This outer body is only with us for the duration of our physical life. The Bible teaches us that those who belong to Jesus will receive a new body after this body comes to its end. Though we will have a new body, we will have the same soul. We are becoming who we will be forever; it is time to work on our soul now.

Roots:

The roots of a tree must be healthy. If you poison the roots, then the tree will not be able to extend itself to reach the nutrients of the soil; eventually the tree will wither and the tree will die. So it is with our inner being...

As Paul wrote a letter to the church in Ephesus he prayed for his friends and wrote:

> *"I pray that from his glorious, unlimited resources he will empower you with* **inner strength** *through his Spirit. Then Christ will make his home in your hearts as you trust in him. Your roots will grow down into God's love and keep you strong. And may you have the power to understand, as all God's people should, how wide, how long, how high, and how deep his love is. May you experience the love of Christ, though it is too great to understand fully. Then you will be made complete with all the fullness of life and power that comes from God."*
>
> **—Ephesians 3:16-19** *(emphasis added)*

From Paul's prayer, we learn that inner strength comes from God. It comes from being in God's presence, trusting God's words and leaning on God's promises.

We also learn that GROWING INWARDS is of extreme importance because it is the act of understanding God's love. It is the experience of feeling God's love. It is the confidence of standing in God's love. We *must* have inner strength because we cannot go without God's love.

We come to inner strength through anchoring our minds, hearts and beings to God's love. We must know God's love. We must accept God's love. We must be rooted in God's love.

When our roots are solid, when we are strong on the inside, then we will be fruitful on the outside. We will be complete and full. We will live in the love of God and live out the power of God.

Inner strength is more important than outer strength.

So how fit are you? Do you need to start exercising your interior? Why not do some right now?

MEDITATE:

So now I am giving you a new commandment: Love each other. Just as I have loved you, you should love each other. Your love for one another will prove to the world that you are my disciples.—**John 13:34-35**

Dear children, let's not merely say that we love each other; let us show the truth by our actions.—**1 John 3:18**

Don't be selfish; don't try to impress others. Be humble, thinking of others as better than yourselves. Don't look out only for your own interests, but take an interest in others, too.—**Philippians 2:3-4**

Let there be no sexual immorality, impurity, or greed among you. Such sins have no place among God's people. Obscene stories, foolish talk, and coarse jokes—these are not for you. Instead, let there be thankfulness to God.
—**Ephesians 5:3-4**

MY THOUGHTS / PLAN OF ACTION

_____
_____
_____
_____
_____
_____
_____
_____
_____
_____

TODAY'S DATE

_____

GROW INWARDS day **FOUR**

IDENTITY

My name is Michael Ayer Acker, son of Timothy Grant Acker and Maggie Aileen Acker. I am an Acker. It is part of my identity. I have a passport with an awful picture that confirms my identity. I have a driver's license with a cheesy grin that proves my claim. I also have a social security card. There is no picture on this one; according to this card I am only a number. But I know the truth: I'm a face, with a name, with a family, with a background, with a job, with dreams, and I guess, also with a number...

Who are you?

Take a moment and send me an email with just a statement of who you are. Include your name, background, picture, family, dreams, positions, social security number and any relevant credit card numbers.

Why not?

Because we know what could happen if we gave away every thing about us. If we did, someone could steal our identity...

That's a weird thought. Someone can steal your identity? Steal your money, I can understand. Pretend that they are you, I can understand. Steal your identity, that's impossible. Only you can really be you.

But what is you?

You are not your number. That is simply how the government keeps track of your money so we can pay taxes. You are not your aging-changeable face, even though we spend so much time thinking that is who we are. You are not your family, though they contribute to your genes, what you do, and how you behave. You are not your background. The Bible says that if you are in Christ then you are a new creation and that the old you is gone. (**2 Corinthians 5:17**).

So you must be your activity, your position, and your job... because that is what you have heard ever since you were little. :

"[*YOUR NAME*], what do you want to *be* when you grow up?"

You were asked this in school, at family functions, and by your friends. You responded: "I want to be an astronaut." "I want to be the President." "I want to be a princess." "I want to be a GI Joe." (At least that's what I said.)

So we grow up thinking that who we are is what we do. And we wage our self-worth on our performance. We compare our efforts and productivity with others to see how valuable we are. We pride ourselves when we accomplish a lot and we loathe ourselves when we cannot seem to be able to do anything. In the midst of all of our activity, we lose sight of our true identity...

Your activity is *not* your identity. It never was. It never will be. You activity is simply your activity. That is it. It is what you do and have done. It is not who you are and who you will be. Your identity is only found in who God created you to be…

God's child.

> *But to all who believed (Jesus) and accepted him, he gave the right to become children of God.*

—John 1:12

Outside of understanding that you are God's child, you will never find complete peace in who you are. God made me to be me. That is the only person I can be. I need to know this, live this, and act this. I want to be the best me that I can be. I will try to grow my soul, my skills and my strengths. And even though I admire you, I can't be you. Even though I appreciate the qualities of another person, I can't be that person. Even though I can learn from a great leader, I can't be him. I can only be me.

I'm beginning to see that this is okay. Because God made me to be me, and He only has one me.

God made you to be you. I wonder if you are trying to be someone else. I wonder if you are having an identity crisis. I wonder if your identity is a slave to your activity and productivity. I wonder if you are not really being you.

Stop it.

You are a human being. Stop acting like a human doing. Stop being someone else. Stop being a *slave* to some expectation from some person who is not God. Stop the identity crisis and know:

God made you to be you.

> *So you have not received a spirit that makes you fearful slaves. Instead, you received God's Spirit when he adopted you as his own children. Now we call him, "Abba, Father." For his Spirit joins with our spirit to affirm that we are God's children.*
>
> **—Romans 8:15-16**

That's a truth to know.

Memorize it. Meditate on it. Then live it out.

THINK ABOUT IT:

What would happen if you lived out this truth? What would happen if you didn't compare yourself to anyone or measure yourself by anything? What if you just decided to be the best child of God you could be?

MY THOUGHTS / PLAN OF ACTION

_____

_____

_____

_____

_____

_____

_____

_____

_____

TODAY'S DATE

_____

GROW INWARDS   day FIVE

TO REALLY, REALLY KNOW

There are several different levels of schooling. There is Pre-school, Kindergarten, Elementary, Secondary, Graduate, Post Graduate and Doctoral Studies. Amongst these levels there are various tracks to take and thousands of different degrees to obtain. That's not all though. There are vocational training programs, adult-education programs, seminaries, online learning, correspondence studies, home school co-ops and many more.

We do not lack for options in schooling.

How is it that, in the middle of so many forms of learning, we seem to really *know* so little?

This is illustrated in Jay Leno's *Jaywalking* TV segment. Jay wanders the streets of New York accompanied by a TV crew; he quizzes random people about the history of the United States, geography, and basic politics. In return, the random person spews random bits of nonsense proving how little they know.

Beyond Jay Leno is the TV show *Are You Smarter Than a 5th Grader?* The mere title of the show is a sad statement on our learning as a nation.

More personally... I was recently looking through some secondary school books and was amazed at how much I had forgotten. What is the capital of Kentucky? When did Hawaii become a state? What is the biggest state in the US? How many Presidents have we had? What year did we land on the moon? Or what year did the Roman Empire end?

At some point in time, I learned all these facts. At some further point in time, I forgot them.

(Thanks to writing this, I've reacquainted myself with the answers to the questions: Frankfort, Kentucky. August 21st 1959. Alaska. 44 Presidents. 1969. Trick question on the Roman Empire; the short answer would be 476 AD.)

We learn and we forget so much. Yet there are others things we never forget. Riding a bike, the seasons of the year, our birthday, the first time you said "I love you" to your spouse, basic arithmetic, where we grew up, the name of our best friend from childhood... there are so many details that we never forget. Even elderly people with severe Alzheimer's have certain memories that breakthrough the disease.

I believe we forget so much of what we learn because we never knew it. It was not part of us. Maybe we heard it. Maybe we were familiar with it. But we did not *know* it like we know the names of our favorite childhood pet.

See, as there are different levels of schooling, there are also different levels of knowing.

1st LEVEL: INSPIRATION.

When we first start to learn something it intrigues us, it informs us, it hits our conscious mind and we grasp it. But we do not know it. This could be hearing something on the History Channel about a famous President. "Hmmm... Theodore Roosevelt was nicknamed Teddy because he refused to kill a bear even though he was a tough guy." Interesting...

We are inspired. But we do not *know*.

2nd LEVEL: FAMILIARITY.

We have heard the information before, we have read it, it has been taught to us and it is starting to stick in our mind. This is a fun stage of learning. It is not just a factoid that we have heard, it is something we are beginning to own. This could be when a kid comes home from school and excitedly recites the 50 states to his Mom: "Mom! Mom! I learned the 50 states!" The learner is still excited at this level, but without going to a deeper level...

...in one year it will be forgotten.

I think this is where many Christians are with the Bible. They are familiar with the Bible. They have been inspired, they were taught or they read it, then time passed, and they forgot. Why? Because they didn't *know*.

3RD LEVEL: BOREDOM

When I was in elementary school, the first month of each year was boring. All we did was relearn what we learned the year before. We practiced multiplication again. We rehearsed the states again. We looked at dead frogs again. It was repetitious and boring. It was also important. The BOREDOM level is actually only deep familiarity. We know the lesson, but we don't *know* the lesson. So the teacher re-teaches the lesson to the class in order to get the information deeper into the student.

This is when the actor repeats their line for the one-thousandth time. On the first reading, the script was interesting. On the 10th practice the actor was very familiar with the script. Several months in to rehearsal, though, the actor is tired of the practice and just wants to perform.

Unfortunately, I think many churches never get to this stage. As a preacher, I can start to feel uncomfortable with teaching the same thing again and again. But unless the actor keeps on repeating and keeps on practicing, the actor will never become the person they are portraying. This third level of knowledge is essential. Next time you hear a spiritual truth that you have heard before, lean in. If you are tempted to become bored, listen all the more. Next time you read a familiar passage from the Bible, slow down. If you are tempted to skim it, focus all the more. Get past your boredom and let the truth sink deeper.

4ᵀᴴ Level: KNOWLEDGE

Knowledge, wisdom, and understanding. This is where you and I want to be. This is where you own the words, the information and the experience. It is part of you. Even if you go a decade without writing, the moment you pick up a pen the ink pours forth in a handwriting style unique to you. Even if you go twenty-five years without a bicycle ride, the moment that you mount it, your legs will start motoring you down the road. Why? Because, it is part of you. You *know* it.

That is how we are to know God. That is how we are to know His truth, His words, and His promises. This is why we do the discipline of scripture memorization.

Get past mere inspiration, move beyond familiarity, grow through boredom and come to knowledge. That is what it means to GROW INWARDS.

> *By his divine power, God has given us everything we need for living a godly life. We have received all of this by coming to **know** him, the one who called us to himself by means of his marvelous glory and excellence. And because of his glory and excellence, he has given us great and precious promises. These are the promises that enable you to share his divine nature and escape the world's corruption caused by human desires.*
>
> *In view of all this, make every effort to respond to God's promises. Supplement your faith with a generous provision of moral excellence, and moral excellence with **knowledge**, and knowledge with self-control, and self-control with patient endurance, and patient endurance with godliness, and godliness*

with brotherly affection, and brotherly affection with love for everyone.

The more you grow like this, the more productive and useful you will be in your knowledge of our Lord Jesus Christ. *But those who fail to develop in this way are shortsighted or blind, forgetting that they have been cleansed from their old sins.*

—**1 Peter 1:3-9** *(emphasis added)*

ACTION:

Make a plan to make Scripture memorization part of your life.

MY THOUGHTS / PLAN OF ACTION

_____
_____
_____
_____
_____
_____
_____
_____
_____
_____

TODAY'S DATE

_____

week FIVE: GROW OUTWARDS

God is a giver. God gives life, love, joy, help, friendship, work… and on and on. God is a giver. God does not give just a little bit; God gives *everything*! God gives Himself. God is generous. GROWING OUTWARDS is the discipline of **generous giving.** We are not made to keep God's gifts to ourselves. We are made to be like God; we are made to be generous. So grow your soul to become like God and give!

GROW OUTWARDS   day ONE

A TALE OF TWO GIVERS

A while ago, someone who visited one of our church gatherings invited me out to lunch. The day came and I showed up for lunch. Surprisingly, this gentleman had invited others of the church leadership as well.

My heart sank. What is this man going to say? What is this about? Am I going to have to confront this man? Who is he?

The leadership team and I sat around the table and realized that the price on the menus were on the expensive side of dining. Our host preempted our price consideration, encouraging us to get whatever we wanted. He was going to cover the expense. "Great, but what's the catch?" my suspicious mind enquired.

After the meal, the man got down to business, "I want to make a donation to your church and to your ministry. How much money do you need to accomplish your goals and vision?"

Uhhhh... Blank stares. Surprise. Bewilderment. This was not what I was suspecting. After some awkward silence, we regained our composure and mentioned several projects and goals. Right there, the man added up all the costs on his phone, pulled out his checkbook, wrote us a check and handed it to me across the table. With the check in my hand, he said to me, "Mike, let me know when you finish the first project. I'd love to be there where your vision is accomplished."

Time passed, and the first project was completed. He came to our celebration. We publicly gave thanks and we looked forward to our next goal.

Just a little while after our celebration, a woman dropped by my office. I remember her because she drove up in a beat-up minivan loaded with her full family. The van sadly puttered up. This thing had seen better days about twenty yeas ago.

She came in, and I expected that she would be requesting some assistance. Instead, she apologized that she had forgotten to tithe that week and handed me a check. Then off she went. I do not usually personally receive checks, but she didn't want to leave the kids in the car so I made an exception. Before putting the check in the giving kiosk, I noticed that her tithe was for just a bit over ten dollars.

The next day, I saw this same woman walking to the grocery store with a couple of kids behind her and one in front of her in the stroller. I pulled over in my car and greeted her and the kids. "What are you guys up to?"

"We're on the way to the store?"

"Oh? And for a little exercise too, eh?"

"Haha. No, the van broke down yesterday and my brother-in-law's friend can't fix it until next week…"

One man came and gave a large amount. He blessed the goals of the church and received recognition from people.

One woman came and gave all that she had. She blessed God with her heart and received His recognition.

This is my modern day parable. These stories did *not* happen to me, but something similar did happen to Jesus:

> *Jesus sat down near the collection box in the Temple and watched as the crowds dropped in their money. Many rich people put in large amounts. Then a poor widow came and dropped in two small coins.*
>
> *Jesus called his disciples to him and said, "I tell you the truth, this poor widow has given more than all the others who are making contributions. For they gave a tiny part of their surplus, but she, poor as she is, has given everything she had to live on."*

—Mark 12:41-44

Is it wrong for "many rich people" to put large amounts of money to the construction of a church? To support a ministry? To further a good cause? To help the goals of the church?

No. They have surplus, and out of their surplus they are able to bless and encourage others. That is a great action to take.

Is it wrong for the "poor widows" amongst us to give what she has to help others?

It depends.

When some Bible historians read this passage with the widow, they note that the reason she is giving to the temple is because the temple authorities are exploiting her. They have built up a massive building that requires them to resort to unrighteous actions such as guilting givers to give. As such, what does Jesus say about the temple? In the following chapter Jesus predicts the downfall of the temple system.

Let me re-ask the question: Is it wrong for religious leaders (or any type of leaders) to guilt the "poor widow" to give in order to help their cause? Yes.

Now, look at the other side of the story. What if the widow wants to give? What if the widow wants to grow outwards? I know of people who have so little, and yet they give so much. I have seen people who do not have much make a Thanksgiving basket to give so that another family can have more. I have witnessed someone who needed financial help who still gave rides to someone needing transportation. I have heard of African villagers preparing meals for visitors using up all their resources. It seems to me that the people from these stories and this widow wanted to give.

Let me ask the question once more: Is it wrong for the person who has little to give to something they feel inwardly compelled to help? No.

So what should you and I do?

Create a surplus and give to the mission of Jesus.

Entrust your provision to God and give to grow your heart.

Here is what Paul says about giving to the church in Corinth.

> *You must each decide in your heart how much to give. And don't give reluctantly or in response to pressure. "For God loves a person who gives cheerfully." And God will generously provide all you need. Then you will always have everything you need and plenty left over to share with others. As the Scriptures say,*
>
> *"They share freely and give generously to the poor. Their good deeds will be remembered forever."*

—2 Corinthians 9:7-9

That's pretty clear.

Decide to give. The Bible gives the guideline of the tithe, the special offerings, and the gifts to the needy.

But don't not give in to pressure. Do not allow guilt to guide you.

God will provide. Like the widow, trust God to provide for your needs (not wants, needs). You will have enough left over to share.

Create a financial surplus through wise management and work hard so that you can give to God's mission.

Give generously. It will take care of others and it will grow your heart to become more like God.

QUESTIONS:

How can you actively grow outwards:
Do you need to start tithing or increase your giving?
Is there some cause, project, or missionary you can give to?
Do you have a way to give to those in need?

MY THOUGHTS / PLAN OF ACTION

_____
_____
_____
_____
_____
_____
_____
_____
_____
_____

TODAY'S DATE

_____

GROW OUTWARDS   day TWO

A FAMOUS VERSE

This is one of the easiest traps to fall into: believing that what you have is for you.

We have all kinds of excuses for falling into the trap:

> "I worked hard for this. I did this thanks to my skills and work ethic."
>
> "My parents gave this to me. It is my right."
>
> "Everybody lives like we do. I am just keeping up with others."
>
> "The media made me do it. I am a victim to consumerism."

There are biblical responses to each one of these excuses (and any other excuses you can make up.)

> Even your ability to work is from God.
>
> All good gifts come from heaven.
>
> Do not forget the unfortunate.
>
> Stop blaming; own up to you own sin.

It is not about *you*. What you have is not about *you*. The money that you earn is not just for *you*. God did not bless you solely for *you*.

One of the most blessed people in the Bible was the man, Abraham. He had a close friendship with God. He knew the will of God. He had a great relationship with his wife. He was still virile in his older age. He had a son who carried on his legacy. He was rich. He had servants. He was successful. He was respected. His enemies feared him. He had loyal companions, consistent friends, and a good life. He was able to enjoy all these blessing through a long healthy life. The man was blessed.

But it was not about him.

> *"This is what the LORD says: Because you have obeyed me and have not withheld even your son, your only son, I swear by my own name that I will certainly* **bless** *you. I will multiply your descendants beyond number, like the stars in the sky and the sand on the seashore. Your descendants will conquer the cities of their enemies. And through your descendants all the nations of the earth will be* **blessed**—*all because you have obeyed me."*
>
> **—Genesis 22:16-18**

My guess is that if you are reading this, you are very blessed. You are blessed with housing, food, family, friendships, some income, possessions, schooling… and the list goes on. We are so blessed in so many ways, and yet we often assume that we have a right to it. We act like we have a right to beautiful homes, to landscaped cities, to safe schools, and to great weather. We naturally assume that it is our divine right to have good health, security, safety, freedom and all the things that we enjoy. We often forget that most of the world is barely struggling to survive.

Let me just put this into perspective.

If you have food in your refrigerator, clothes on your back, a roof overhead and a place to sleep, you are richer than 75% of all the people in the world. You are in the top 25%.

If you have any money in the bank, some money in your wallet, or some spare change in a dish someplace you are among the top 8% of the world's wealthy. You are richer than 92% of the people in the world. You are blessed.

If you have never experienced the danger of battle, the loneliness of imprisonment, the agony of torture, or the pangs of starvation, you are already ahead of five hundred million people who have experienced those things.

You are blessed. But it is not about you. Abraham was blessed to be a blessing to others. His family, provision, lifestyle and good standing were given to him so that he could be a blessing to those around him and to the generations after him.

His upright life was to display God's order and loving intentions to the community around him.

His power and might were given to him and his family to take care of the oppressed and to bring justice.

His wealth was given to him to take care of his family and the people who came to him for care. Beyond taking care of people, he tithed to the high priest Melchizedek and gave offerings to God.

His loyal family was given to him to be agents of God's love to the world throughout all the generations. Through Abraham, God blessed the world with Jesus.

It was not about Abraham and it is not about you.

The question is, what are you going to do with your blessing?

ASK YOURSELF:

What are you going to do with your blessing?

MY THOUGHTS / PLAN OF ACTION

_____
_____
_____
_____
_____
_____
_____
_____
_____
_____

TODAY'S DATE

_____

GROW OUTWARDS   day THREE

THE DAVE RAMSEY IN ALL OF US

I was drowning in debt. I had no plan. No help. And no clue. For example: I was using my credit card, debit card, and check book to pay for all my expenses and wants. Meanwhile, as I spent, I kept track of my money with my mind. Amazing how ineffective my mind could be…

Opening up my web browser one day, I clicked on my bank's website to do one of my periodic checkups…

negative $400

I am not a violent man. I do not cuss or kick black filing cabinets. That day I did. The chair was thrown back, the cabinet was dented, my foot was hurting, and I was glad that nobody was around me at my church office.

That was it. No more. I had had enough. I was so stressed. I was not making lots of money. I was living on peanut butter and Jelly sandwiches. I was trying to pay off college, repair my car, get rid of credit card debt. But after months of living frugally, I would splurge on something stupid. Then my checks would bounce and the overdraft fees would kick in… $40 + $40 + $40 + $40 + $40… $400 of debt.

Along with my swearing, I prayed to God. Shortly afterwards, I came across Dave Ramsey's audio book, *The Total Money Makeover*. I listened to it three times in one week, and with "gazelle intensity", I started working on a plan to get out of debt.

Six months later…

No debt. Less stress. Better food. Planned spending. Inexpensive lodging. And I started giving more (just a little bit).

While I was in debt, I had a hard time giving. Why give when I owe on a credit card? Why give when I needed it? Why give when I had to use my money just to live?

Can you relate?

According to many statistics, the average household debt is $15,000.

Did you know that there are more than a million bankruptcies filed per year in America?

It is hard to give when these are the statistics. It is even harder when this is your reality. When I was in debt, I did not often tithe to God, I tipped the church a couple dollars. When I was in debt, I did not trust God, I relied on Visa and MasterCard. I told myself, "I will start to give when I get out of debt."

Have you told yourself something like that? "I will give when I get everything in order." Here is the truth: No, you won't. The average giving for a Christian is a mere 2.8%. When you get out of debt, when you make more money, it just gets harder to give.

While I was in debt, I was a servant to my lenders through my poor planning.

> *Just as the rich rule the poor, so the borrower is servant to the lender.*
>
> **—Proverbs 22:7**

When I got out of debt, I was a servant to my money through my greed.

> *No one can serve two masters. For you will hate one and love the other; you will be devoted to one and despise the other. You cannot serve both God and money.*
>
> **—Matthew 6:24**

The day came when I had no debt. I started to give more (but just a tiny bit more). Money was my master, and I needed another money makeover.

Back to Dave Ramsey I went. This time I did his Financial Peace University. I came to see that I was serving myself instead of serving my God. I repented and started to give faithfully. I started to grow in giving. Over time, I started to give to other areas. I started giving more. It became fun to give.

I learned that I could truly help others with my giving. I learned that one of the reasons to get out of debt was so that I could give and make a difference. Isn't that more exciting than owning one more DVD or buying two more coffees?

Are you in debt with your credit cards, your car, your poor planning? Are you a servant to your lenders?

Get help. Get intense. Get out.

Are you selfish with your money? Do you give less than 10%? Does your money simply stay with you? Are you a servant to your money?

Give to your church. Give to God's Mission. Give somewhere. Grow outwards away from your selfishness and self-centeredness. Give generously and grow your soul to become like God.

RECOMMENDATION:

There are several financial programs available through churches, workplaces, colleges and online. I have only been to Dave Ramsey's Financial Peace University. I highly recommend finding a program and faithfully going through it: daveramsey.com

MY THOUGHTS / PLAN OF ACTION

_____

_____

_____

_____

_____

_____

_____

_____

_____

TODAY'S DATE

_____

GROW OUTWARDS   day FOUR

SIM CITY

As a teenager I loved to play the computer game Sim City. My best friend would come over and he would watch me playing the game for a couple hours. Sometimes, I let him control the game, but most of the time I kept it to myself.

Fast-forward fifteen years. My friend had moved to England and was getting married. I flew out to go to the wedding. My dad joined me for a European trip. It had been a decade since they had seen each other and they started to catch up:

> *Dad:* "So what do you like to do for hobbies?"
>
> *Friend:* "I do some photography and editing. My fiancé and I like to go on walks or go dancing. Oh, and I like playing Sim City."
>
> *Dad:* "You and Mike were always on the computer playing that video game."
>
> *Friend:* "Yeah, yeah. We were always on the computer. But Mike played and I watched. So just a little while ago, I bought the game to see why Mike liked playing it so much and now I'm hooked."

Fifteen years after my selfish-teenage-non-sharing-video-game-ways, my dad comes over to me and chastises me for being so selfish. "Mike, that was a jerk thing to do." A bit belated, but rebuked nonetheless.

My dad's comment caused me to reflect on my teenage ways. I had so much: video games, music, computer, gadgets, early Internet subscriber... I had so much when all of this was so new. I wanted people to see what I had but not to use what I owned. I was greedy and did not want to share.

Who would have thought that fifteen years later, my best friend would still remember how greedy I was? Who else remembers what I withheld from them?

How will people remember *you* in fifteen years?

Will they laughingly reflect on your greed or commend your generosity? Will they remember how you withheld hospitality from them or how you welcomed them in to your life? Will they critique you for being stingy or will they praise you for how you made a difference through your generosity?

The earliest church was so affected by the life-giving generosity of Jesus that they shared everything.

> *All the believers were together and had everything in common. They sold property and possessions to give to anyone who had need. Every day they continued to meet together in the temple courts. They broke bread in their homes and ate together with glad and sincere hearts, praising God and enjoying the favor of all the people. And the Lord added to their number daily those who were being saved.*
>
> **—Acts 2:44:47**

These followers had the heart of Jesus. Like their Lord, they gave generously. That is how they are remembered two thousand years later.

I was remembered as a stingy immature teenager. They are remembered as people who shared with anyone in need. How will you be remembered?

ACTION:

Do an inventory of what you own and what you can do. Then share your stuff and skills with others. Give something away. Do something for somebody. Share.

MY THOUGHTS / PLAN OF ACTION

_____
_____
_____
_____
_____
_____
_____
_____
_____
_____

TODAY'S DATE

_____

GROW OUTWARDS   day FIVE

BEYOND THE GOSPEL

As Christians, the most important treasure we own is the experience of the Gospel:

> *For God loved the world so much that he gave his one and only Son, so that everyone who believes in him will not perish but have eternal life.*
>
> —John 3:16

As followers of Jesus, the most important mission we have is to give this good news to others:

> *And then (Jesus) told (his followers), "Go into all the world and preach the Good News to everyone. Anyone who believes and is baptized will be saved. But anyone who refuses to believe will be condemned."*
>
> —Mark 16:15-16

The Gospel is life giving, life transforming and life altering. The Gospel is the difference between light and dark, between life and death, and between heaven and hell. The Gospel is Good News. It is amazing news. It is God's message of grace and truth to us.

Yet it wasn't enough for Paul to share just the Gospel...

Because we loved you so much, we were delighted to share with you not only the gospel of God but our lives as well.

—1 Thessalonians 2:8

Paul wrote that he did not want to share *only* the Gospel. Somehow that was not enough. He could not just give them the gift and then move on. He had to give himself as well. Wow.

One of my heroes is Carlos Maralinera. He is a pastor of a church in Mazatlan, Mexico. He moved there from Mexico City responding to God's call. He wanted to preach the Gospel. So he did. He started a church. Each week, he preached the Gospel on Sunday. He went around the neighborhood and preached the Gospel. He visited the prison and preached the Gospel. Everywhere he went, he boldly gave people the message of Jesus.

But it was not enough for Carlos to just give the Gospel. He had to give more. He had to give his life to these people even if that meant he needed to be in the prison several times a week so he could talk with the murderous inmates. Even if that meant he needed to spend countless hours putting together feeding centers to bring the community together for meals. Even if that meant he and his wife had to work far more than the forty-hour workweek. He just had this burning passion to give the Gospel and even beyond the Gospel...

It is so important to become a giver. We need to *give* the gospel by telling people about Jesus. We need to *give* money generously to the mission of Jesus so that people hear about Jesus. We need to *give* help to people so that there aren't obstacles that keep people from believing in the good news.

But don't stop there. Share the gospel *and* share your life. Give generously and live generously.

As you get a hold of your finances and understand the call to give money to the mission of Jesus… watch out! If you are not careful, your gifts to the mission can keep you from giving yourself to the mission. Giving money can become a substitute for giving your time to others, your skills to God's church and your heart to people.

Do not be content to go half way; learn from Paul. Give the Gospel and give generously so that the Gospel is given. Then go beyond the Gospel and give yourself.

CONSIDER:

How much time do you give to helping, loving, and serving people outside your immediate family and friends? Does this need to change?

MY THOUGHTS / PLAN OF ACTION

_____

_____

_____

_____

_____

_____

_____

_____

_____

_____

TODAY'S DATE

_____

week SIX: GROW UPWARDS

Since the beginning, humanity has thought of God as living above us. Men and women have raised their eyes to the heavens to call out to God, worship God, and to seek God. GROWING UPWARDS is joining with generations of seekers to meet with God through requests, through conversation, and for worship. This is the discipline of **prayer.**

GROW UPWARDS   day ONE

MY BEST FRIEND

Who is your best friend? Do you have one?

Now, if you are used to the classic Sunday School answer, you may be tempted to dismiss this question by simply saying, "Jesus." After all, as a kid I thought that was the answer to every class question. "Who made Adam?"—Jesus! "Why did Noah build the arc?"—Jesus! "How did David defeat the giant Goliath?"—Jesus! "How can you get better grades at school?"—Jesus?

So who is your best friend? Jesus… That is more difficult to decide fully than it is to declare verbally.

My first best friend was Gabe. Gabe and I were kindergarten buddies. But he told my girlfriend Anna (she didn't know we were dating) that he loved her. That ruined our friendship. Then there was Zach, then Aaron. Aaron and I were close, until we tried to kill each other with branches after fighting over who would get the cool stick. We were 15 years old …

… No, just kidding, we were kids. As quick as we started fighting, we overcame it to become even better friends.

Moving to Mexico, I moved to new friendships. Andy and I became great friends. Secretly, he was my best friend, but I didn't have that number one place in his friendship list for a while. I still remember clearly when we were around a fire pit sharing life stories with a large group of people; Andy stood up to share what he was grateful for and it included his best friend—Mike. Then he moved.

From Andy to Luis. Isn't it interesting how you can have friends that are completely different? They were opposites. Andy and I played basketball. Luis and I rollerbladed.

From Luis to Chava. He and I became friends after Luis' enemies wanted to beat me up in sixth grade. It is good to have a friend who carries a bat around and who is not afraid to use it.

From Chava to Ricardo. Ricardo and I did everything together: concerts, sports, studying, work… in my lifetime he is my number-one best guy friend. Eventually, he moved to England. We wrote, e-mailed, called and visited. Years later we were part of each other's weddings… but it was not the same. We went from being best friends to good friends with great memories.

From Ricardo to _____.

That's it. For twenty years I had a *best* friend. From then on, I had good friends, great friends, acquaintances, sports friends, church friends, family friends, work associates, car pool buddies… but no best friend.

That is where I was in my life when my dad met me at my college and we went out to eat. Over dinner I told him about my friendship dilemma. He listened and nodded, and when I was ready, he interjected, "Mike, maybe God hasn't given you a best friend because *He* wants to be your best friend."

That sounds so deep. Or does it sound so cliché?

I listened to my dad, I nodded, and when we were done, I went home to think about it. It has been ten years, and I am still thinking about it.

How can you be a friend with God? It is possible. Abraham became a friend of God (**James 2:23**). Perhaps God even became Abraham's best friend. They were close. They loved each other. They worked well together. Sure the relationship, was extremely lopsided, but God is okay with that. He condescends to our level in every other area even taking on our sin, so why not come down to our level for friendship?

Think about your friendships for a moment. If you are a guy, who are your great guy friends? Do you have any? Do you have a best friend? If you are a girl, who are your girl friends? Whose friendship do you cherish, and with whom do you fully share yourself?

Think about what created those friendships: Connection. Mutual understanding. Fun memories. Time together. Love. Respect. Good conversations.

These are all elements of good friendships. And you can have that with God. Amazing. It truly is possible to become *best* friends with God.

It has been ten years since my dad told me that perhaps God wanted to be the one in the best friend slot. I didn't know how to go about it, so I told God something like, "God… ummm… you heard what my dad said. It's true I don't have a best friend, that role is open in my life, and I would like to *you* to become my best friend."

Nothing happened.

At least right away.

It takes time.

Time passed. I improved in my connection with God. I grew in my understanding of God. Some of my best memories are times I was aware of God's presence in my life. Over the years, we have spent more hours together than I have with any other person. I love God. I know He loves me. I respect, revere, am in awe of God. He knows me. And we always, always have great conversations…

… even when I don't hear from God… even when I'm mad at God… even when I don't voice my thoughts… even when I am apologizing… even when whatever… God receives as prayer my thoughts, words, cries, pleas, apologies, anger, thanksgiving, and praise.

Prayer is what makes your friendship with God.

Prayer: conversation, hearing through the Bible, discerning God's voice, talking about all areas of life, words shouted out, silent pleas for help. Prayer.

How do you become better friends and eventually *best* friends with God? Prayer. He is open. He has already come down to our level. He is just waiting for you and me.

It has been twenty years since I asked God to be my best friend. It is taking time, but it is happening. Year by year, month by month and day by day, God is filling that role in my life. I have had many best friends, but *he* is the best one of them all.

Now to you: God wants to be *your* best friend.

Sounds like a cliché, and it can be, if you let it. Or it can be a truth so deep that it transforms all other friendships.

QUESTION:

Is God your friend? Or is He just an acquaintance? Your Savior? The Lord? What conversations do you need to have with God right now?

MY THOUGHTS / PLAN OF ACTION

_____
_____
_____
_____
_____
_____
_____
_____
_____
_____

TODAY'S DATE

_____

GROW UPWARDS   day TWO

DON'T STOP 'TIL YOU GET ENOUGH

In 1979, Michael Jackson wrote the song, "Don't Stop 'til You Get Enough." Since then, countless musicians from Juan Luis Guerra to Jay-Z to U2 have covered the song. After he wrote the award-winning song, he explained that the song's appeal is the combination of the melody, the new feel, and that the song can apply to anything involving persistence. So, let's apply it to prayer. After all, persistence and prayer go together even better than "U" & "2."

When you pray, how do you pray? Do you make a request and then move on? Do you pray about something only to forget the words you prayed? Do you give thanks to God one day, and feel entitled to blessings the next? How persistent in prayer are you? Do you give up praying for those whose situation is helpless? Do you keep on praying for those areas that need God involved?

As you read the following parable from Jesus, think about how persistent you are with prayer:

> *"There was a judge in a certain city," he said, "who neither feared God nor cared about people. A widow of that city came to him repeatedly, saying, 'Give me justice in this dispute with my enemy.' The judge ignored her for a while, but finally he said to*

himself, 'I don't fear God or care about people, but this woman is driving me crazy. I'm going to see that she gets justice, because she is wearing me out with her constant requests!'"

Then the Lord said, "Learn a lesson from this unjust judge. Even he rendered a just decision in the end. So don't you think God will surely give justice to his chosen people who cry out to him day and night? Will he keep putting them off? I tell you, he will grant justice to them quickly! But when the Son of Man returns, how many will he find on the earth who have faith?"

—Luke 18:2-8

There is so much in this parable: the justice of God, the sovereignty of God, and the election of God's people. Though this parable touches on these areas, what is Jesus' main point? It's found in the first verse.

One day, Jesus told his disciples a story to show that they should always pray and never give up.

—Luke 18:1

Could it be any clearer that God desires us to GROW UPWARDS in prayer? It is so important that at the end of the parable, Jesus equates our persistence with faith! It makes sense if you think about it. If you believe that God answers prayers, if you take Jesus' teaching seriously, if you have God as your friend, if you have faith in a God who is powerful and who loves you… then doesn't it make sense to pray?

What if the prayer is unanswered? Well, how much faith do you have? The more faith in your relationship with God, the more you go to Him in prayer. Likewise, the more you pray to Him, the more your faith with grow.

So what are you praying for? Have you given up on your friends? Have faith–pray.

Do you need a job? Do you need provision? Have faith–pray.

Are you lonely, sick, doubting, troubled? Have faith–pray.

Do your family or friends need a miracle? Have faith–pray.

Like the song: Don't Stop 'til You Get enough…

Don't stop praying. Keep at it. GROW UPWARDS–pray.

MEMORIZE:

"Never stop praying."—***1 Thessalonians 5:17***

MY THOUGHTS / PLAN OF ACTION

_____
_____
_____
_____
_____
_____
_____
_____
_____
_____

TODAY'S DATE

_____

GROW UPWARDS   day **THREE**

...

Silence…

What is the quietest place you know?

The wilderness–maybe. Home–perhaps. The bus–definitely. When you take the city bus, there is no place more silent. It is eerie. There are people in every seat. Each person is looking straight ahead, ignoring all the others. Have you been on that bus? It is unsettling. It seems like there is a rule that no words may be spoken.

Imagine you are on this silent bus, and for some reason you could suddenly hear the thoughts of everyone on the bus. The noise would be maddening:

"Here comes my stop." "I wish I had taken Driver's Ed." "This guy smells." "What's for dinner tonight?" "I wonder what the Pastor is talking about this week." "Money. Money. Money." "Why isn't anyone talking?"

Even though no words are voiced, the thoughts would be in abundance.

And… God can hear each one…

At the age of eighteen, I was working as a busboy for a local restaurant. I was working on memorizing scripture. So, I chose one of the easiest verses to remember:

> *"Never stop praying."*
>
> **—1 Thessalonians 5:17**

Short verse: Great way to start memorizing.

Short verse: Extremely hard to obey. How can you "never stop praying?" I can't walk around the restaurant muttering to myself. But I wanted to obey it. I wanted to try it. I was committed. As I worked my job, I prayed and prayed and prayed. I prayed for the people I worked with. I prayed for my family. I prayed to make money (just being honest).

But are these effective? Does God *hear* my thought prayers. Do they count as a 'prayer time'?

Turn to the book of Nehemiah, chapter two.

Nehemiah was a cupbearer to the King. Nehemiah had been praying to God about the condition of Israel. It was on his heart and in his prayers. One day, as he was serving the King, an opportunity showed itself:

> So the king asked me, "Why are you looking so sad? You don't look sick to me. You must be deeply troubled."
>
> Then I was terrified, but I replied, "Long live the king! How can I not be sad? For the city where my ancestors are buried is in ruins, and the gates have been destroyed by fire."

The king asked, "Well, how can I help you?"

With a prayer to the God of heaven, I replied...

—Nehemiah 2:2-5

Nehemiah then laid out his vision to the King. The King granted Nehemiah's request to rebuild the walls of Jerusalem. The King further bought into Nehemiah's vision by giving him resources to do the work.

Nehemiah "never stopped praying". At home, he had times of prayer where he verbalized his thoughts, praises, and requests. At work, he continued his prayers silently in his mind, knowing that God hears every thought equally as his spoken words.

Here is my goal:

- I want to pray continuously while at work, while out for coffee, while struggling to overcome sin, while around my family, while out at a restaurant...

- I want to have times of prayer that are intentional, focused and just between Father God and I.

- And I want these two types of prayers to be contiguous, continuous and constant.

Isaac and I use to work together as pastors. Sometimes, on Tuesday mornings, we would jump in the car and drive down to get coffee talking together the entire time. When we got back, we'd sit down at the conference table, pull out agendas, and move into an official meeting where we would talk about plans and preparations.

In the car and at the coffee shop, Isaac and I talked about anything and everything. The flow of our words was random, and it often included anyone we'd come into contact with.

In the office, Isaac and I talked with intentionality and with purpose. It was an official time to talk and it was focused.

From the coffee shop to the conference table, the conversation was contiguous, continuous and constant.

How about it? How's your prayer life? Do you need to start praying everywhere, all the time? How about a time of prayer that is focused and intentional? How about a life of prayer where the conversation never ends? That is my goal. How about making it yours?

Oh. And the next time you are on the bus… turn the silence into silence that matters. Turn it into prayer.

TODAY:

As you go about today, take some moments to pause and pray. When the moment is over, remember that God is WITH you and though the **moment** *of prayer is over, prayer is not.*

MY THOUGHTS / PLAN OF ACTION

_____
_____
_____
_____
_____
_____
_____
_____
_____

TODAY'S DATE

_____

GROW UPWARDS   day FOUR

SEEING WHAT GOD SEES

Reticular Cortex: a small part of your brain that is responsible for making your brain more aware of different goals, opportunities and information that you have set your mind on.

Here is how it can work:

During college, my trusty 1983 Honda Prelude died. I was cruising down the freeway in the 60–70 MPH range when my transmission blew. After some loud revving and gradual slowing, I ended up cruising down the freeway at 25 MPH. That is when I decided that, after three years of multiple problems, it was time for a new car.

I bought a 2000 Daewoo Lanos. I had never seen one before in the Seattle-Metropolitan area. I was excited to be potentially driving the only Daewoo in Washington. That is when my reticular cortex kicked in. Before buying my new car, Daewoos were not on my mind. After purchasing my Lanos, I saw Daewoos everywhere. My neighbors had one. I parked next to one in Bellevue. I got stuck in traffic next to a car identical to mine. Since I owned a Daewoo, my mind was aware of Daewoos and my eyes started seeing Daewoos.

The reticular cortex serves as a mental radar, and I am sure you have seen it activated in your life many times as well.

When you decide that you want a big-screen TV, every house or store you go to happens to have *your* TV. Every commercial or ad you come across points you to the big screen TV that you want. It is on your mental radar.

When you set your mind on a goal to eat less, you capture the scent of delicious food everywhere. Every conversation you enter seems to be an invitation to eat dessert. Food is on your mental radar.

When you start enjoying a specific song or band, you hear the music at every restaurant, every friend's home, and on every radio station you turn to. The music is on your mental radar.

Because of the reticular cortex, you begin to see what you decide is important to you.

Prayer can activate the reticular cortex better than any personal goal, selfish desire or great idea ever can. When you come to God in prayer, your priorities shift, your desires change, and your goals are altered. The more time you spend praying, "Not my will but Yours be done", the more God will place His priorities, desires and goal on your mind. As prayer becomes a lifestyle, so does God's life become your mission.

Through prayer, you will see what is important to God.

Through prayer, you will see God-opportunities to be a part of.

Through prayer, you will see people you are called to serve.

Through prayer, we begin to see what we could not see before. In 2 Kings 6 Elisha has been continually thwarting Aram's military advances by prophetically informing the Israelite king of their plans. So the King of Aram sends a great army to capture the prophet Elisha.

Can you imagine waking up one morning to see that your city is surrounded by enemy troops just so that they can get to you? How would you respond? Well, it depends on how well you can really see.

> *When the servant of the man of God got up and went out early the next morning, an army with horses and chariots had surrounded the city. "Oh no, my lord! What shall we do?" the servant asked.*
>
> *"Don't be afraid," the prophet answered. "Those who are with us are more than those who are with them."*
>
> *And Elisha prayed, "Open his eyes, LORD, so that he may see." Then the LORD opened the servant's eyes, and he looked and saw the hills full of horses and chariots of fire all around Elisha.*

—2 Kings 6:15-17

Elisha was a man who prayed. Elisha saw what God saw. The servant of Elisha was like most people: concerned with circumstances, going about life without supernatural awareness and unable to see God's involvement.

Who are you more like?

TRY THIS:

Pray about every area of your money. Pray to pay off your debt. Pray for the needs you have. Pray for the people you can help. Pray for the church you tithe to as you tithe to the church. As you pray about every area of your money, God will begin to open up your eyes to how He would have you manage money. Your needs will be taken care of, stress will decrease, and you will see opportunities where you can make a difference.

Pray for the five to ten closest people in your life. Pray for them daily. Pray for their health. Pray for them to know Jesus. Pray for needs. Pray for their relationships. As you pray for these close friends and family, God will begin to open up your eyes to see how you can love them and be an encouragement to them. You will think about them more often, you will desire to call them more frequently, and you will be aware of opportunities where you can make a difference.

I could go on with other areas of prayer, but the principle is the same. Pray, and let God activate your mental radar, your reticular cortex, so that you may become a Godsend to the people God puts in front of you.

MY THOUGHTS / PLAN OF ACTION

_____
_____
_____
_____
_____
_____
_____
_____
_____
_____
_____

TODAY'S DATE

_____

GROW UPWARDS   day FIVE

BE WITH

What is the point of prayer?

That is too broad of a question. Jesus himself prayed for several different reasons: He blessed water to make wine, He prayed for healing, He praised His Father through prayer, He prayed for God's will, He expressed the feeling of separation, He blessed little kids, He asked for unity…

Jesus prayed for several different reasons. These were effective prayers. They accomplished great miracles, saw great results and produced answers that the public could see.

Here is one interesting example:

> *"One day soon afterward (healing on a Sabbath) Jesus went up on a mountain to pray, and he prayed to God all night. At daybreak he called together all of his disciples and chose twelve of them to be apostles."*
>
> **—Luke 6:12-13**

Jesus had been drawing a crowd every time He taught. Hundreds of people were following Jesus. Then came the time for Jesus to choose the Apostles for His mission. He went off by Himself and prayed to God the Father all night. What did He say? Did He debate whether Peter has the right stuff? Maybe He argued with His Father about including the tax collector? Probably, He discussed Judas Iscariot at length... "Do you really think this man should be on the team... he's going to betray me... he's going to steal money from the mission... he's not good for the twelve... You know, we are going to have to replace Him..."

Jesus prayed all night long. In the morning, Jesus chose the twelve apostles, and more than two thousand years later, the Church is continuing to grow and appoint new leaders for the mission. I would say that Jesus' night of prayer was very productive! That gets me excited and motivated to pray. I want to see results! I want to get God's wisdom! I want to make an impact on this world (for Jesus, of course)! I want that type of productive prayer!

Now, consider **Luke 5:15-16:**

> "...despite Jesus' instructions, the report of his power spread even faster, and vast crowds came to hear him preach and to be healed of their diseases. But Jesus often withdrew to the wilderness for prayer."

Sometimes Jesus prayed and everyone saw immediate results. Sometimes Jesus prayed and great productivity resulted. But, *often* Jesus simply *withdrew to the wilderness for prayer.* No fantastic results. No great production. He simply got away to be with God the Father.

What did Jesus do on these other times? What did Jesus accomplish? What did Jesus produce?

A while back, my Dad invited me to spend a night on his boat with him down where he lives. I drove nearly three hours in traffic during the dinner hour to arrive very hungry at his doorstep (if you can say that about a boat). We ate. Went out for some music. Talked until bedtime. Got up in the morning to have breakfast. Then it was back on the road to go back home. Two more hours of driving. During the drive, I captured a stray thought: "That wasn't very productive…"

"Productive"? Is that the word to describe friends or family? Do we need to accomplish something with friends to be friends? Do we need to see results after going out with our siblings? Do we need to produce when we are with our parents?

No.

When I visit with my sister at a restaurant, the whole *point* of going out is to *be with* my sister. When I spend the night at my dad's, the whole *point* is that we have a relationship. When I take my wife out on a date, the whole *point* is to enjoy each other's company.

And when I pray, the *point* is to be with the God who loves me and whom I love in return.

Does prayer bring about results? It might. Can prayer produce great miracles? Absolutely. Should we pray for tangible effects? Yes. Jesus prayed for all of these and so should we. Just do not start thinking that it is the *point* of prayer.

Prayer is more than production.

Prayer is more than results.

Prayer is more than answers.

Prayer is when you are with the Father. It is when you have faith that He is with you, not against you. It is when you humble yourself to recognize His worth and bring Him worship. It is when you are quiet before Him and simply trust Him. Prayer is when you are with God: quiet, conversational, sad, happy, humble, inquisitive, hurting, requesting… and beyond all these, prayer is when you are *with God in relationship*.

Be still, and know that I am God!

—Psalms 46:10

QUESTION:

When and why do you primarily pray?

MY THOUGHTS / PLAN OF ACTION

_____
_____
_____
_____
_____
_____
_____
_____
_____
_____
_____

TODAY'S DATE

_____

week SEVEN: GROW DOWNWARDS

It is too easy to think too highly of ourselves. If we do not take our thoughts captive and remind ourselves that we live for God, then we will end up thinking that God exists for our comfort. GROWING DOWNWARDS is the discipline of **fasting**. It reminds us of our need for God more than entertainment, activities, or even food. Fasting reminds us to humble ourselves before God and live for His glory instead of our own.

GROW DOWNWARDS   day ONE

THIS MOVIE IS NOT ABOUT YOU

There are some things you just know you need to do. They are a given. They are expectations. You will eat. You will sleep. You will breathe. You will talk. You will work. You will die. These are common to every single human being. Every one of us will give into these common experiences.

For the Christian, there exists another set of expectations, common experiences, and given observances: Pray. Give. Fast. There are others, but these three show up as a trio in Matthew chapter six.

Matthew 6:2,3	"When you give…"
Matthew 6:5,6,7	"When you pray…"
Matthew 6:16,17	"When you fast…"

Several years ago, a lady called my office. "What happened to my son at youth group?" Those are not the words you want to hear at the beginning of a conversation. I was not there that night and I had not heard anything so I was at a loss. She went on to confusingly describe some spiritual experience that her son had felt during church. This opened up a conversation about life with God, and soon we were praying for her and her son. This woman was not yet a disciple of Christ, yet she was already praying.

Although we still need to grow upwards through prayer, this act is something that most followers of Christ and many outsiders automatically engage in.

After a couple months of coming to our Sunday services, a man who was new to faith in Christ asked me to join him for lunch. We had a great Mexican food feast and then came the point for the appointment. "Pastor, am I supposed to pay the church 10% of my money?" This opened up an opportunity to talk about growing outwards through the discipline of generous giving. When we left the restaurant, he left with a plan to grow in this discipline.

Another evening, I found myself talking to a devoted Christ-following couple. This couple had over 20 years of following Christ, reading the Bible, and participating in the local church. Our conversation turned to a recent challenge that I had given the church to fast from food. This couple had never been asked to fast, never taken on a fast, and had never understood the need or call to fast.

There are three "When You" statements:

- "When you pray…" Christ followers and even outsiders engage in Prayer.

- "When you give…" Regular churchgoers are regularly called upon to give.

- "When you fast…" How is it that this expectation has gone unobserved so many times, in so many churches, for so many Christ followers? After all, Jesus did say "when you…" not "if you…" or "should you desire to…" or "you don't have to but you might want to consider…"

Read these words of Jesus and consider them at face value:

*One day the disciples of John the Baptist came to Jesus and asked him, "Why don't your **disciples** fast like we do and the Pharisees do?"*

*Jesus replied, "Do wedding guests mourn while celebrating with the groom? Of course not. But someday the groom will be taken away from them, and then **they will fast**."*

—Matthew 9:14-15

*And **when you fast**, don't make it obvious, as the hypocrites do, for they try to look miserable and disheveled so people will admire them for their fasting. I tell you the truth, that is the only reward they will ever get. But **when you fast**, comb your hair and wash your face. Then no one will notice that **you are fasting**, except your Father, who knows what you do in private. And your Father, who sees everything, will reward you.*

—Matthew 6:16-18

Jesus clearly expected those who follow him to fast: "Then they *will* fast." Jesus also gave clear instruction for whom we fast: "No one will notice… except for your *Father*." Jesus gave a clear command for his disciples to engage in the discipline of fasting.

Why?

When we fast, we choose to go without something we desire, something we do, or something we need. Then we fill that longing with contentment, we fill that time with prayer and we fill that absence with God's presence.

When we fast, we humble ourselves.
Instead, we recognize the Glory of God.

When we fast, we get the focus off of ourselves.
Instead, we turn our attention to God and His mission.

When we fast, we abstain from something good.
Instead, we trust that God will fill us with something better.

When we fast, we stop being the main character in 'our' movie.
Instead, we realize that this movie of life is *His*.

When we fast, we grow downwards so that God is recognized in our lives, acknowledged in our successes, and honored by our humility.

FOLLOW-UP:

There are countless resources on fasting: books, articles, websites, sermons and seminars. Go beyond these devotions and research a fuller biblical understanding of why, how and when to fast. Then do it.

MY THOUGHTS / PLAN OF ACTION

_____

_____

_____

_____

_____

_____

_____

_____

_____

_____

TODAY'S DATE

_____

GROW DOWNWARDS   day TWO

THE BOW

There are several variations of bowing in oriental countries. Hands by the side–bow. Hands together–bow. Right fist, left palm–bow. Right fist, left enclosure–bow. Kneeling, hands in triangle–bow.

Each form of the bow derives from cultural traditions, practical reasons, and honorable intentions. Through all the variables, there is one common trait that is found in each bow: the back of the neck is always exposed.

As you lean forward, you show vulnerability–trust & surrender.

In leaning forward, you acknowledge power–respect & honor.

By bowing, you lower yourself–humility & submission.

There are many parallels between the Fast and the Bow.

Subjects of the oriental kingdoms would bow before their emperors. They would show trust, surrender, respect, honor, humility, and submission. They realized that their life was under the care and control of their ruler.

We need to realize that our life is under the care and control of our Ruler. Yet, we so easily ignore this. See, the Bible shows us that Jesus is our confidante, our counselor, our healer, our brother, our savior, our redeemer, our mediator, and our friend. We can approach Jesus unashamed, boldly, confidently, joyfully, continuously, privately, or publicly. We can come to Jesus with our doubts, fears, concerns, celebrations, trials, regrets, plans, and even our trivialities.

This is all true.

It is also true that God is the creator of the entire universe. His breath is the beginning of your life. From one utterance He started the cosmos. He stands outside of time. He understands all, sees all, and knows all. He is beyond description. His power is outside of scientific possibilities. His mind created the laws that our minds try to find. Only He knows the plans He made. God raises up rulers and topples empires. God is sovereign, supreme, and the single entity from which all other entities derive. God is One and God is Three. He is the only Being to be one–yet more than one. God is the Father. God is the Son. God is the Spirit. God the Son stepped into His creation. God clothed himself in flesh. Fully God–Fully Human. God became one of us, yet He did what only God could do. Perfection. Resurrection. Ascension. Jesus sent HIS Spirit to live inside us. God is everywhere and God is right here. Jesus stands at the right hand of God the Father. Jesus is coming again. The first coming was in humility; the second coming is in *glory*. Jesus will judge the entire world. He will put an end to sin. He will put away the devil. And then... every knee *will* bow.

The list of God's attributes goes on and on. (**Revelation 4. Exodus 19. Job 38-41. Isaiah 6. Ezekiel. Daniel 7.**)

It is right for the subjects of God's reign to show trust, surrender, respect, honor, humility, and submission to our Ruler. Fasting is an appropriate way to do so. Fasting is a way to remember who God is and who we are.

After Job's incredible encounter with God, he replied:

> "*I know that you can do anything, and no one can stop you. You asked, 'Who is this that questions my wisdom with such ignorance?' It is I—and I was talking about things I knew nothing about, things far too wonderful for me. You said, 'Listen and I will speak! I have some questions for you, and you must answer them.' I had only heard about you before, but now I have seen you with my own eyes. I take back everything I said, and I sit in dust and ashes to show my repentance.*"

> **—Job 42:1-6**

When Job came to understand who God is, it drove him to his knees. He bowed before the Creator. He sat in ashes and showed his repentance.

When God formed the nation of Israel and gave them laws through Moses, He instated a yearly ritual of repentance called Yom Kippur (the day of Atonement). This yearly reminder of God's reign was accompanied by...

Fasting.

Every year the Israelites were commanded to fast so that they would remember to trust in God, to surrender to God, to respect God, to honor God, to show humility before God and to submit to the God who creates life, sustains life, and brings fullness to life.

It is good to ponder, to wonder, and marvel at who God is. He is your friend, and He is your Dad. He is also King of the Universe. Humility, respect, and honor are due.

It's time to bow.

PRAYER:

Take some time to humble yourself before God. Acknowledge Him, thank Him, praise Him, kneel before Him and honor Him.

MY THOUGHTS / PLAN OF ACTION

_____
_____
_____
_____
_____
_____
_____
_____
_____
_____

TODAY'S DATE

_____

GROW DOWNWARDS day THREE

MORE THAN PERSONAL

For a brief time, I decided I was going to become extremely physically fit. I had heard about the 300-workout regimen and decided to do it. I wanted to bulk up, fill out, and be beyond fit. Three to five times a week, I went to workout. I did it mostly for myself. It felt good. It was personally important. Then, over time, I lost my enthusiasm and simply stopped.

For quite a while, my friend has been physically fit. He has done several different regimens and has continued to do them over and over. He is strong, he is filled out, and he is fit. He works out several days of the week and does not let up. He enjoys it. He likes the outcome. It is personally important to him.

Working out is a personal hobby for my friend, but he also does it for more than personal reasons. He is a trainer. He owns a training business. He trains for himself, but he also trains himself as a role model for others. My guess is that he would workout regardless of his profession; he is just that type of guy. At the same time, his profession gives him a constant reminder to keep up his physique. His workout is both deeply personal and it is more than personal. He uses his fitness to serve others.

The act of fasting is extremely personal. Fasting is not meant to be done to impress others. Jesus commanded that His disciples not let on to anyone when they fasted. It is to be done personally, just between God and you.

When King David sinned by committing adultery, he took on a personal fast of repentance. He humbled himself before God and prayed to God for forgiveness. In his written prayers he writes *"Against you, and you alone, have I sinned"* (**Psalms 51:4**).

When Jesus traveled to the desert to prepare for ministry, he engaged in a personal forty day fast. He went alone into the wilderness to commune with His Father.

Time and time again, people fast for personal reasons: healing, repentance, preparation, prayer, and many more. In the days of the prophet Isaiah, many in the nation of Israel routinely fasted for personal deliverance. This would have been fine except that they were not troubled by the plight of those around them. They took no concern that there were people around them wearing rags, living on less than food stamps and sleeping without warm homes.

So God sent Isaiah on a mission. He gave Isaiah a message for His people. God wanted His people to have His heart. He wanted them to fast for more than personal reasons; he wanted them to fast for the spiritual needs of others and to bring them to acts of love.

> *You humble yourselves*
>   *by going through the motions of penance,*
> *bowing your heads*
>   *like reeds bending in the wind.*
> *You dress in burlap*

> *and cover yourselves with ashes.*
> *Is this what you call fasting?*
> *Do you really think this will please the LORD?*
>
> *No, this is the kind of fasting I want:*
> *Free those who are wrongly imprisoned;*
> *lighten the burden of those who work for you.*
> *Let the oppressed go free,*
> *and remove the chains that bind people.*
> *Share your food with the hungry,*
> *and give shelter to the homeless.*
> *Give clothes to those who need them,*
> *and do not hide from relatives who need your help.*

—Isaiah 58:5-7

When we fast, we grow in humility and we grow in receptivity to God's will. God's will is that you and I have love and concern for others so much so that it causes us to do good for others.

When we fast, it is personal. It is also beyond personal. It drives us to turn the arrows of our hearts outward so that we bring healing, hope, and help to those around us and around the world.

When *this* becomes our attitude, God responds with this promise:

> *Then your salvation will come like the dawn,*
> *and your wounds will quickly heal.*
> *Your godliness will lead you forward,*

*and the glory of the LORD will protect you from behind.
Then when you call, the LORD will answer.
'Yes, I am here,' he will quickly reply.*

—Isaiah 59:8-9

So, fast…

Fast for whatever personal reason you may have. Are you in need of healing? Fast and pray. Do you find yourself in awe of God? Fast and praise. Are you in the middle of difficulty? Fast and pray. Are you overwhelmed by guilt? Fast and repent. Do you see immaturity in your life? Fast and pray. Do you want to plan for the future? Fast and prepare.

Fast for whatever personal reasons you may have, but do not let it stop with simply you. Pray for the healing of others. Ask God to reveal himself to your community. Help others through difficult situations. Walk in confession and forgiveness with others. Help others grow through immaturity in their life…

… and prepare for a life of service where your good actions are more than just personal.

ARROWS-OUT FAST:
Is there somebody you need to fast for and pray for?

MY THOUGHTS / PLAN OF ACTION

_____

_____

_____

_____

_____

_____

_____

_____

_____

_____

_____

TODAY'S DATE

_____

GROW DOWNWARDS   day FOUR

GET READY FOR _____

How long do you take to get ready in the morning?

How long did you take to prepare for your career?

How long do you spend making dinner?

Each person reading this will vary widely in their response. Some people take years in preparation for their career. Others just happen upon their employment. Some men take no time to get ready; others take longer than my sister ever did. Some girls spend hours making the most elaborate meal. Some take out the cup-o-noodle and they are good to go. Everybody is different, but many times, the outcome follows a similar pattern. Generally, the more time you take to get ready, the more prepared you will be.

Think about what this means for the follower of Christ who wants to engage in God's mission and who wants to become *holy*. If you want to be the person that God intends you to become (like Jesus) then it is going to take time. It is going to take time spent with God. It is going to take days and weeks and months of journeying with other Christ followers. It is going to take years of participating in God's mission, praying for God's heart, and obeying God's words.

It is going to take time.

But preparation takes more than time. It also takes commitment, heart, and intentionality.

How long do kids spend in school? Is every graduate equally prepared for life after school? Why not? Why do some people excel after graduation? Several reasons: Diligent effort in classes. Hard work in studying. Good counsel from teachers and parents. Wisdom gained from experience and listening.

Some people take the time needed for preparation, yet they don't invest any effort, work, or diligence. As a result, even when the time is put in, the results do not show. Time to grow was allowed, yet no fruit is manifested.

Think about what this means for the followers of Christ who fill American churches. Thousands and thousands of people have put time into becoming more like Jesus. They have spent hours reading the Bible... but maybe they did not do what it says. They have spent the hundreds of days in fellowship... but maybe they never built a relationship that went beyond meals, studies, and activities. They spent the years as Christians... but instead of maturing to become like Jesus, they simply grew old in the church seats.

Does this describe you?

Are you spending time as a Christian but not putting your heart, soul, strength and mind into becoming one?

You must love the LORD your God with all your heart, all your soul, and all your mind.

—Matthew 22:37

But don't just listen to God's word. You must do what it says. Otherwise, you are only fooling yourselves.

—James 1:22

To become holy, more like God, it will take you time and intentionality. As you take this time and as you put your heart into it, you will find that you are ready to engage in God's mission as He shows you opportunities all around. Fasting is an important part of this.

Consider Esther.

Teenage girl. Beautiful. Despised Jewish ancestry in the land of the conquering nation Babylon. Raised by her cousin since her parents died. Picked to be part of the beauty pageant to potentially become the next queen. Moved into the King's palace. Won the King's affection. Became Queen of Babylon. Hidden Jewish identity. Heard of a plot to wipe out the Jews. Her cousin Mordecai challenged her to use her position to do something about it:

> *Mordecai sent this reply to Esther: "Don't think for a moment that because you're in the palace you will escape when all other Jews are killed. If you keep quiet at a time like this, deliverance and relief for the Jews will arise from some other place, but you*

and your relatives will die. Who knows if perhaps you were made queen for just such a time as this?"

—Esther 4:13-14

God placed her in this position for "such a time as this." God had a mission for her. She saw it. But it loomed large in her mind and fears. Yet, she decided to engage the mission. She decided to do something about the situation in front of her. So how did she go about it?

She walked into the king's chamber and demanded to be heard?

She organized a protest?

She raised up an army to fight against her enemy?

She wrote letters and letters and letters?

She took matters into her own hands?

What did she do to get ready to engage in this mission?

> *Then Esther sent this reply to Mordecai: "Go and gather together all the Jews of Susa and fast for me. Do not eat or drink for three days, night or day. My maids and I will do the same. And then, though it is against the law, I will go in to see the king. If I must die, I must die." So Mordecai went away and did everything as Esther had ordered him.*

—Esther 4:15-17

When confronted with a problem, Esther prepared by fasting and praying. Only then was she ready to engage the mission that

God had for her. Her mission was a success. Her victory was commemorated as a national holiday for the Jews (Feast of Purim). As a result, her example has been on display for a few thousand years and to a few billion people. And to think… it started with a fast.

What do you need to get ready for? A big move. A family decision. Choosing your career. Selling your home. Overcoming an illness. Going into vocational ministry. Leading your organization. Having a difficult conversation with your kids.

Each person reading this will vary widely in response. But each of us have areas of life that we need to get ready for. Even if we do not know what that is right now.

So get ready, do a fast, pray, put the time in, and put your heart in it too. Then open your eyes and see what mission God is directing you to.

QUESTION:

What is something you need to fast and pray about?

MY THOUGHTS / PLAN OF ACTION

_____
_____
_____
_____
_____
_____
_____
_____
_____
_____
_____

TODAY'S DATE

_____

GROW DOWNWARDS   day FIVE

DON'T STAY AWAY–COME BACK

There are some things that we should just keep coming back to.

It does not matter how mature we are or how experienced we are, there are some basic practices that we need to weave into the ongoing fabric of our lives. Fasting is one of these.

There is a true and legendary story where Coach Vince Lombardi reminded his Green Bay Packers to keep coming back to the basics. After some frustration with his team, Lombardi had called the players together. He held up a football, "This is a football. These are the yard markers. I'm the coach. You are the players." He continued one by one walking through the most elementary aspects of football.

Who did he tell this to? National Football League players. Professional athletes. Men who have played since childhood, through high school, for college, and now in front of the nation. Hall of Fame Coach, Vince Lombardi felt it necessary to come back to where they all started.

We need to do the same.

God made us. Mankind sinned. Jesus redeemed us. Christ calls us to a life of holiness…

How do we get there?

How do we become more like God?

The Father guides us. The Holy Spirit dwells within us. Christ Jesus instructs us.

There are God-ordained practices that, over time and with commitment, mold us and make us into who we are created to be.

Fasting is one these. It is not a one-time event. It is an ongoing discipline of self-denial that causes us to lean into our Lord. Fasting should be a regular part of our life as followers of Jesus.

Consider the Day of Atonement (**Leviticus 23**). In the life of Israel, the people had a specific time to fast. It was built into the calendar.

Consider Lent. The early church instated a seven-week fast, which called Christians to deny something they deeply desired.

Consider the Apostle Paul. We read that Paul regularly fasted and he taught that it was to be a way of life for Christians (**2 Cor. 11:27, 1 Cor. 7:5**).

Fasting is a practice that God has given to us. As we take the focus off of ourselves and we rely on Jesus, God empowers us so that we can walk through this journey of life with strength and victory instead of being weak and ensnared by sin.

This is fasting.

CALENDAR:

These five readings on fasting are over. You have completed the week, but you have not completed the call to fast. Take out your calendar or take up a sticky note. Make a note to fast in a week or in a month. Put it on your calendar. Do not stay away; keep coming back to the fast.

MY THOUGHTS / PLAN OF ACTION

_____
_____
_____
_____
_____
_____
_____
_____
_____
_____
_____

TODAY'S DATE

_____

week EIGHT: GROW TOWARDS JESUS

It is all about Jesus. Jesus was in the beginning; Jesus will be at the end. He is the Alpha and the Omega. *"Christ is the visible image of the invisible God. He existed before anything was created and is supreme over all creation, for through him God created everything in the heavenly realms and on earth."* (**Colossians 1:15-16**)

It is all about Jesus. It is not about you. So get over yourself and grow. After all, GROWING TOWARDS JESUS is what every **disciple** should do everywhere, everyday, all the time.

GROW TOWARDS JESUS day ONE

WHO YOU SPEND TIME WITH

You become like the people you spend time with.

As a teenager, my parents limited my time with one of my friends, Alex. This annoyed me. Alex was cool. He was fun to be around. He was great at sports, art, music, pop culture knowledge, and most importantly, he was great at talking with girls. Honestly, I looked up to Alex. We were close in age, but still I wanted to be like Alex.

Then the opportunity came. My family was living in Mexico. One year, they gave me the option to live in the United States for two whole months with a friend! I was only in 8th grade, but I knew exactly with whom I wanted to live. Unfortunately, my parents knew exactly with whom they didn't want me to live. We burst into an argument. Vividly I remember my mother's reasoning, "The more time you spend with Alex, the more you adopt his attitude. We don't like the way he treats his parents. And we don't like the way you treat us after you spend time with him." The conversation was over. I stayed in the United States with a family of my parents' choosing. My time with Alex was limited.

In retrospect, I understand. Don't you? Do you have some friends that 'rub off' on you? Did you have an 'Alex' when you were growing up? Have you watched people change and adopt the attributes of those around them? I'm sure you have. We know this. We become more and more like the people we spend time with.

Who are you spending time with?

In the Bible, the book of Daniel tells the story of Daniel (and his friends). Most books of the Bible describe the successes and the sins of the Bible characters. Daniel is unique. Other than Jesus, he is only one of two people whose sins are never mentioned. It's not that he didn't sin. He did. Daniel even mentions that he confessed his owns sins to God in chapter nine. However, the reader never sees any of his sins. Instead, again and again and again the people around him make these types of observations: 'he is wise beyond compare', 'the spirit of the Holy God is in him', 'he is without blame'.

When we read the first six chapters of the book of Daniel, we see a man who is wise, pure, disciplined, honest, courageous, trustworthy, humble, pious, and loving.

How can we have more people whose sin list is eclipsed by their massive character count?

How can we have more Daniels and Danielas?

Your 'Daniel Destiny' depends on who you spend time with. The secret of Daniel is found in chapter six, verse ten: "He prayed three times a day, just as he had always done, giving thanks to his God." You become like the people you spend time with. Daniel spent time with God. He became Godly.

There are all these types of Christian disciplines: fasting, prayer, worship, confession, generosity, reflection, meditation, witnessing, and many more. The point of Christian disciplines is not to simply have Christian disciplines. The point of Christian disciplines is to be with Jesus.

When you journal, you are writing your story with Jesus.

When you pray, you are taking time to talk with Jesus.

When you witness, you are telling people about Jesus (with Jesus alongside you, as seen in **Matthew 28:19-20**).

When you praise and worship, you are recognizing the worth of Jesus.

When you give, you are growing your heart to be more like Jesus.

When you meditate, you are filling your mind with the words of Jesus.

When you reflect, you are quieting your mind to hear the words of Jesus.

The point of Christian disciplines is Christ.

Someday, I will tell my kids what my parents taught me: "Show me your friends, and I will show you your future."

I will ingrain these words into the minds of my kids. Why? Because, you become like the people you spend time with.

FRIENDSHIP LIST:

Who do you spend time with? Take a moment to analyze whether they are influencing you or whether you are influencing them. How about your time with Jesus? Take another moment to think about how your time with Jesus is impacting your life and your friendships.

MY THOUGHTS / PLAN OF ACTION

_____
_____
_____
_____
_____
_____
_____
_____
_____
_____
_____

TODAY'S DATE

_____

GROW TOWARDS JESUS   day TWO

WHERE I LOOK IS WHERE I GO

Do you remember learning how to drive?

My parents took me to get my learner's permit when I was 15 years old. I enrolled in driver's ed. I spent that summer reading the handbook, going to classes, and driving while my mom panicked or my dad shouted. Great summer.

A couple decades later, some of the lessons still run through my mind: the 10 and the 2, hold the wheel firmly in case of a tire blowout, the correct positioning of the mirrors, and look where you want to go.

I remember it as if I was still 15 years old. The instructor stood in front of us. "Don't look at the yellow line. Otherwise, you will drive towards the center of the road. And be careful when you look into your rear view mirror, because you won't have a clear point to focus your driving towards. Even though you need to check your mirrors and notice the cars around you, you want to focus down the road." After some words very similar to this previous quote, the instructor stated very clearly, "Look where you want to go. You will drive towards whatever you focus your eyes on."

I don't know why those words stuck with me. Sometimes I'll be driving down the road and those words will run through my mind. When I learned how to ride a motorcycle, I rehearsed those words as I raced around corners. When I went to England, those words nearly killed me. My eyes focused on the right lane, but my car was supposed to be in the left lane. Dad was riding shotgun and kept shouting, "Get back in your lane!" (I felt 15 all over again)

"Look where you want to go." This is true for learning to drive. This is also true for the direction we drive our soul. Whatever we focus on our sight on we will drive towards.

The author of Hebrews never drove a car, but he knew this truth:

> *"And let us run with endurance the race God has set before us. We do this by keeping our eyes on Jesus, the champion who initiates and perfects our faith."*
>
> **—Hebrews 12:1b-2**

Where you look is where you go.

The Bible tells us that God has set a race of life before us. Life is a journey to travel all the days that we are here. Then, this life takes us on into eternity. Our destination is determined by the direction of our soul. Our direction flows from our focus. How do we steer our soul towards Heaven? "We do this by keeping our eyes on Jesus…" In other words, look to where you want to go.

What are you looking at? That is where your life is headed.

Are you looking at your own achievements, your own success, and your own plans? Then your life is headed towards a life that is all about you.

Are you looking at your previous accomplishments, your former failures, or the 'good ol' days'? Then your life will get caught in the prison of the past.

Are you looking at temporary pleasure, greedy accumulation of goods, and the lust of the eyes? Then you life will have a fun ride… until your consumerism crashes you.

What are you looking at? Wherever you look towards, that is where your life will take you.

Spiritual disciplines are not the focus. Spiritual disciplines are the tools that keep our eyes on Jesus. Spiritual disciplines grow your souls towards God because they lead you to look to Jesus.

You are where you are because of where you looked to in the past. Where will you be tomorrow because you focus there today?

EXERCISE:

Here are some questions to help you discover what you are looking at.
What do you spend your extra money on?
How do you begin and end your day?
What fills your mind throughout the day?
What are some areas you worry about?

MY THOUGHTS / PLAN OF ACTION

_____

_____

_____

_____

_____

_____

_____

_____

_____

_____

TODAY'S DATE

_____

day TWO:
GROW TOWARDS JESUS

GROW TOWARDS JESUS day **THREE**

YOU WILL FAIL. YOU CAN GET UP.

Today, I have good news and bad news for you.

The bad news is that you *will* fall.

The good news is that you *can* get back up.

My wife and I were over at our friends' house. While enjoying our conversation, their son and his friend were running around like wild men (as boys often do). They ran in circles, splashed water, threw balls at each other, and jumped off the deck. *suddenly* they collided. There was a noise. There was a crash. There was a 'bonk' as one head knocked against the other.

The father of the little boy looked over, assessed the situation and gave this wise advice: "Shake it off. You're okay. Get back up."

The Bad news is that you are going to 'bonk' your head too. Someday you will experience the pain of collision. Someday you will crash into problems. Someday you will fall, and you will fail.

The bad*der* News is that this will happen several times. Now, aren't you glad you reading this?

But the bad news doesn't have to stay bad. The good news is that you can get back up.

for though a righteous man falls seven times, he rises again…

—Proverbs 24:19a (NIV)

Even the righteous man will fall! Not just once! The righteous man falls seven times (the number 7 often symbolizes a full measure). Did you hear it? Did you catch it? For every fall, there can be a rise. Even if you fall seven times, you can get back up eight. Fall Seven. Rise Eight.

Everyone falls. Everyone fails. The big question is what do you do afterwards.

When we think about this journey towards Jesus, I give you a caution of two extremes.

1—Falling down—giving up—staying down.

2—While standing up, thinking we will never fall down again.

Proverbs 24:19a inspires us to overcome extreme #1.

1 Corinthians 10:12 cautions us against extreme #2

"So, if you think you are standing firm, be careful that you don't fall!"

The path towards Jesus is lifelong. Let's approach this journey with humility and confidence.

HUMILITY:

Recognizing that we are sinful people who don't have it all together. Knowing that we are shortsighted and that we will err. Having a realistic view of ourselves instead of an inflated view.

CONFIDENCE:

Recognizing that Jesus has conquered the power of sin. Knowing that the God is for us, and with us, *will* help us. Having the Biblical view that God is a good Father who will reach down and say, "Shake it off. You're okay. Get back up"

ENCOURAGE YOURSELF TODAY:

Talk positively to yourself.
Speak encouraging words out loud to yourself.

MY THOUGHTS / PLAN OF ACTION

_____

_____

_____

_____

_____

_____

_____

_____

_____

_____

TODAY'S DATE

_____

GROW TOWARDS JESUS day **FOUR**

WHEN WE EXPERIENCE #FOMO

I missed my 21st birthday party. Completely missed it. It was during my Junior year in college. A bunch of guys from my dorm floor were pumped to have a midweek outing in the university district of Seattle. Although we didn't attend the University of Washington, we decided to celebrate in that area. After all, our town of Kirkland was known for starting the Kirkland brand at Costco; it was not known for fun midweek evening activities. We tossed around some ideas. It was decided that we would hit up the popular improv theatre and then get some burgers afterwards.

The plan was set in motion to celebrate *my* birthday party. We had several hours to spare, so I returned to my room along with my roommate to work on homework.

Studying made me yawn. I decided to 'rest my eyes' (as my dad used to call it). I had plenty of time. Besides, my roommate was in the room. A short while later, I woke up alone in my room. Opening the door to the hall, I saw that the dorms were eerily empty. It was quieter than during finals. These were pre-texting years, so I dialed my roommate:

> "Where are you?"

"Mike, where are *you*? We are in Seattle getting tickets. You have to be here in 15 minutes or they close the door. And they don't let people come in late so they don't disturb the show…"

I wasted some time by furiously asking, "WHY DIDN'T YOU WAKE ME UP?" (It's always someone else's fault, right?)

"I was out of the room and thought you were with someone else. They thought you were with me. We are all here and you'd better get here fast."

#FOMO

With intense fear of missing out on my own birthday party, I sprinted to my 1983 Honda Prelude. Together, Charlie (the Prelude) and I sped across the 520 bridge that separates Kirkland from Seattle. The minutes ticked by as the speedometer ticked up. Illegally parked, I rushed to the ticket booth at the same time that two random girls were speed walking towards the ticket seller. The three of us quickly bonded when we heard the words, "You are too late."

#IMO (I Missed Out)

There are certain people and events that we just want to be with or be at. U2 held a Joshua Tree concert. I had serious #FOMO. When I was in Junior High, my buddy Andy always seemed to be having the time of his life. If I wasn't with him for the ride, then I experienced #FOMO. What about you? When have you gotten anxious because you weren't able to be *there*? A concert. An event. Some friends getting together. With a person who you look up to...

There are certain times, charismatic people, and entertaining activities that we just do *not* want to miss out on.

But... could it be that that #FOMO can actually be a good thing and turn into #fo-MO...

In the Bible, we see Jesus describe a moment when his 12 key disciples were going to miss him. He tells them:

> *"In a little while you won't see me anymore. But a little while after that, you will see me again."*

> **—John 16:16**

Those seemingly vague words caused some serious anxiety in these core followers. They had given up jobs, ambition, livelihoods, and plans in order to be with Jesus. They had been traveling with him for 3 years. *wherever* he went, they went.

> *Perplexed, some of the disciples asked each other, "What does he mean when he says, 'In a little while you won't see me, but then you will see me,' and 'I am going to the Father'? And what does he mean by 'a little while'? We don't understand."*

> **—John 16:17-18**

They didn't want to miss out. They didn't want to miss their friend. They were confused as to why they couldn't be with

Jesus in that moment. They just wanted to be able to hang out with Jesus. They weren't concerned with the mission of Jesus, they were worried about personally missing Jesus.

> *Jesus realized they wanted to ask him about it, so he said, "Are you asking yourselves what I meant? I said in a little while you won't see me, but a little while after that you will see me again. I tell you the truth, you will weep and mourn over what is going to happen to me."*
>
> **—John 19-20**

Jesus was foretelling the historic fact of his impending crucifixion. He was predicting their response: grief, sorrow, intense Fear of Missing Out for everything they had hoped and desired in Jesus.

#FOMO is a trendy hashtag. It is also a real emotion and motivation. Sometimes, #FOMO is just a fun saying we throw out there. Other times, #FOMO is a motivation that causes to us jump onboard instead of waiting for the right time. For fear of missing out on something right now, we can end up missing out on something much bigger over time. To satisfy the need for pleasure in the short term, we can forsake the pleasure over the long term.

#FOMO has led many people to forfeit the future for the moment.

#FOMO has led millions to acquire debts and regrets.

Have you ever sacrificed the Big Picture for the small snapshot you see in the moment? Have you ever done something impetuously that you regretted the aftermath? That is #FOMO gone wrong.

If Jesus had not gone to the cross, then salvation and forgiveness would not have come to us.

If Jesus, the God-man, did not die, then men and women could not truly live.

> *Jesus said, "You will grieve, but your grief will suddenly turn to wonderful joy. So you have sorrow now, but I will see you again; then you will rejoice, and no one can rob you of that joy. At that time you won't need to ask me for anything. I tell you the truth, you will ask the Father directly, and he will grant your request because you use my name."*
>
> **—John 16:20b, 22-33**

If Jesus had not gone away, then we couldn't have had him come close through His spirit.

When the 12 disciples' #FOMO was enacted, the gospel of Jesus experienced incredible forward momentum.

Sometimes, #FOMO is a good thing.

I missed out on my birthday party. My friends were inside laughing and having a great time. #FOMO hit me. Then I looked up from my birthday-pity-party. There were two girls who also missed their outing. The three of us talked and agreed to go over to eat some late night pancakes at IHOP. Conversation came easily. We talked about life, trips, friends, college, hopes, dreams, and regrets. At college, I was preparing to be a pastor. At IHOP, I was practicing being a pastor. There, in that late-night venue, I had the chance to offer God's forgiveness, leadership, and direction in their life. I had thought I wanted to be somewhere else; it turns out I ended up being right where I was supposed to be.

My initial fear that I was missing out turned into this incredible time of forward momentum for their lives through the Gospel of Jesus. My #FOMO turned into some incredible Gospel #fo-MO (my semi-cheesy hashtag for forward momentum).

Weak pun aside: Are you so focused on what you *might* be missing out that you actually *will* miss out on something bigger?

Are you so focused on being blessed by Jesus that you are missing out on doing the work of Jesus?

Are you so focused on the temporary that you are missing out on the eternal?

Or perhaps, do you crave the immediate comfort of Christ that you are ignoring the cause of Christ?

Don't base your actions on #FOMO, look for what creates some serious #fo-MO.

LOOK AT YOUR CALENDAR:

Take a moment to look through this upcoming year of your life. What can you intentionally miss out on now so that you have a great impact for the future? Forfeit something now (coffee, going out, movies, personal hobbies) so that you can have something bigger and better in the future (mission trip, time with family, sponsor kids).

MY THOUGHTS / PLAN OF ACTION

_____

_____

_____

_____

_____

_____

_____

_____

_____

_____

TODAY'S DATE

_____

GROW TOWARDS JESUS   day FIVE

HOW DO I GET THERE FROM HERE

When you find yourself in an unfamiliar location, you find yourself asking the question, "how do I get *there* from here?"

Of course, now days we have Siri and Alexa to help us. We pose the question to our phone, "Directions to my desired location?" What happens next? One of two things: we get directions… or Siri-Alexa responds, "You need to turn on location services."

What are location services? It's the feature in your phone that allows the phone to track where you currently are. So, here is my soul question for you, "Where *are* you?" I don't care where you physically are. I really don't. You could be reading this at home. You could be reading this in the bathroom (then I really don't want to know). You could be reading this at work (on a legitimate break, hopefully). You could be reading this as you drive… (*'don't'*–just read it later!). I really don't care where you are physically, but I do care where you are spiritually.

My hope for you is that you get closer to Jesus. It is *there* that I want to direct people. It is *there* that I want to go personally. It is *there* that I pray for people to journey towards. It is *there* that motivates me to write this. But, how do you get *there*? It starts by turning on the locations services of your soul. Where are you right now? Where is "here"?

- Are you in the habit of connecting with Christ everyday?

- Do you find yourself buried in doubt?

- Have you forgotten your first love? (As talked about in Revelation chapter 2).

- When you turn off the distractions, what comes to mind?

- If someone asks, "How are you, really?" what is your honest answer?

- What relationship do you think about the most? You and yourself? Someone you chase after? People's expectations? God's love for his children (including you)?

Questions like these clarify the question of "Where is here?"

Take a moment. Turn on the location services of your soul. Be honest with yourself. Where is your "here"?

From *here*, we can begin to travel towards *there*. Spiritual disciplines become the step-by-step directions towards this new direction. Depending on your *here*, different disciplines take priority.

If you find yourself in a season of grief, then fasting can focus that pain to bring healing.

Are you isolated? Then developing relationship through groups, relational confession, and fun friendships should be the way to steer your life story in this season.

Is your life one big, fun, joyful adventure? Consider jumping into generosity. Share your joy with others!

Do you struggle with discovering your current location? Then begin to examine, journal, and reflect.

I can direct you to general spiritual disciplines. I recommend all of these ancient Christian actions. Each will guide you and grow you. They will get you moving towards Jesus. I can direct you in a general direction. Only *you* can take these generalities and make them specific. How? By questioning yourself, you can locate yourself. By analyzing your current location, you can discover what steps you need to take to get moving onward, upwards, and towards Jesus. He is the big *there* that I pray you travel towards. He is your goal. Grow your soul more like God. Grow your soul towards Jesus.

Some questions to help you discover your next step:

- What do I need to take a break from to refocus my energy and time towards God?

- Is there a tool that I could use to help me study the Bible? (a commentary, good English translation of the Bible, reading plan, devotional, etc.)

- Who can I talk to that would give me outside perspective into my life?

- When was the last time that I *knew* I was in the center of God's will? What led to that moment?

- What spiritual discipline (giving, fasting, prayer, study, confession, etc.) jumps out at me?

As you search your soul, your location services will turn on. Then you will know the direction you should travel.

One last step:

Move. Drive. Go forward. Do it! Siri can tell me where to go, but she can't make me get there. That is up to me. So it is with you. Take an action.

DO *IT* TODAY:

MY THOUGHTS / PLAN OF ACTION

_____
_____
_____
_____
_____
_____
_____
_____
_____
_____

TODAY'S DATE

_____

CONCLUSION:
"I WILL TAKE MY NEXT STEP."

So what's next for you?

Maybe start back at the beginning with examination? Pick up the Gospel of John to meditate on the life of Jesus? Spend some time in prayer? Get involved in a group where you can grow like Jesus with friends?

Perhaps you want more chapters such as the ones written here? I had additional writings that didn't fit here, but if you would like you can get more at https://book.mikeacker.com/grow. Whatever it is, before you close this book, think through what your next step will be.

For me, I desperately wanted to get unstuck. I didn't want church to be a routine or an obligation. I was sick and tired of being sick and tired. Thankfully, I believe God called me back to do the things I did at *first,* including coming back to this book.

Wherever you go from here, join me and take intentional steps to become more like God. That is our goal. For each person the needed discipline may be different. Do not be someone else, be you. And grow your soul to become more like God.

YOU CAN BECOME GOD-LY

My friend was wrapping up a sermon to the church where he was the pastor. He passionately emphasized his concluding point: "Don't you realize that you are gods!? You are gods! *You are gods!* You *are* gods!" Over and over he proclaimed his concluding point.

Wait a minute. Did he really say that? Yes. However, that is not what he meant. He meant to say, "Don't you realize that you are God*'s*!? You are God*'s*! *You are God's!* You *are* God*'s*!" He was very correct in emphasizing whose we are, although it sounded like he was making an incorrect statement about who we are.

You and I will never become a god. Never. We are creation, not creator. We are limited, not limitless. There are some pop psychology books about unlocking your true self and discovering your inner deity. Those are false books that will blow up your ego and deviate you from God's true direction. Don't go there.

You will never become a god. You can become like God. You can become godly.

My son is small. In the morning, he stands on a stool and watches me get ready for work. I reach for the toothbrush. He watches me and then he reaches for Mom's toothbrush. He vigorously brushes, spits, and then taps the toothbrush on the sink just as I do. Then, as I shave, he transforms the toothbrush into a razor. He scrapes his face, runs it under water, and taps it again on the sink. He takes small actions that make him feel he is becoming like me. Every day, I see this. Again and again, he strives to become like me. I love it, but he will never be me. Even though we bear resemblances, he will always have a different DNA. He will never be me, but as he takes small actions, these take him closer to becoming like me.

We can never be a god, but we can take small actions that take us closer to being like God. We can become more loving. We can gain more insight and wisdom. We can grow in generosity and charity. We can become truth-tellers and grace-givers. We can increase in faith, boldness, and courage. We can help, encourage, strengthen, admonish, correct, and support others.

We can become like God.

You can become more like God.

In college, I read the classic book by Dietrick Bonhoeffer, *The Cost of Discipleship*. As a young man, I devoured the content and then I became depressed. I wrote in the margins, "Who can do this?" The portrait of a disciple is so perfectly illustrated in the book that I found myself comparing my reality with a Biblical ideal. Part of my personality makes me always want to be *there*. I want to have *arrived*. I read something and I want to do it *all*. I hear a teaching and I want to *fully* embrace it. So, I despaired as I read that book; I knew that I couldn't skip to the end of my soul's journey; after all, "Who can do this?"

It turns out that I can. Twenty years later, many of the attributes that I desired have become part of how others describe me. I am still growing. I am not *there* yet, and at times I've taken steps back. With my eyes on Jesus, I am taking steps to get *there*. And that is the key to this entire book: Take your next step.

WHAT IS YOUR NEXT STEP?

Some friends of mine used the book you are holding when I gave them a rough draft a while back. They began to embrace a couple of these spiritual disciplines. They fasted as I recommended. They examined their soul and journaled as I suggested. Some time passed, and they told me that they were re-reading the devotional anecdotes in this book. After a second read, they were inspired to grow in generosity. Their second steps were not the same as their first steps.

As time progresses and you climb towards godliness, some of these disciplines will become more important during different seasons of your life. When I was twenty-two, I was not a generous person. A mentor challenged me in this area of life. I took that step. It was a *huge* step for me at the time. I was working two jobs. One was very early and the other kept me going until very late. Generosity was not an easy action for me to take. By the grace of God, I aimed my soul in that direction and began to grow my soul in that direction.

As I took steps outward, I started to understand what it meant for God to love the world so much that he *gave* His son. As I kept stepping towards generosity, my heart grew and grew. The more steps I took, the easier it became to walk in the footsteps of Jesus. Eventually, giving a tithe was easy for me. It became a routine. Over time, there were different seasons where generosity would re-emerge as my big next step: adopt missionaries, sponsor more kids, give 1% more every year, etc. Each of those actions were new steps in the direction of generosity. With each step, my heart grew to become more like the most generous person in all history: Jesus.

Then, with burnout and tiredness, I backtracked. After years of good financial management, we ended up in debt. My empty soul and empty bank accounts led to taking many steps backwards. As God began to heal me and restore me, I began to give again. I took new steps of renewed trust. With each new step, I aim towards being like Jesus. That is my goal. That is wholeness and holiness.

Throughout the years, different themes and different directions have begged for my attention. I have taken steps in intimacy with God through prayer. I have taken humbling steps with others through confession. I have ventured into the forgotten steps of fasting. And, unfortunately, there have been times where my soul has backtracked. There have been seasons where I ignored prayer, embraced sinful slipups, and even distanced myself from God. You can probably relate. It has not been a constant journey towards Jesus. Thank God that salvation doesn't rely on me! Each time God has graciously steered me back to Him.

Through His strength I have gotten back up and started forward again. You can too. At times, I have even had to relearn steps. My friend Pat was immobilized when he jumped into a river and hit a rock. He had to relearn how to walk. During different seasons, I have felt like Pat in my spiritual life as I relearned different disciplines: prayer, study of scripture, fasting, journaling, and others.

BEGIN AGAIN

You might not be where you once were, but you don't have to be where you are right now. You can take the next step with Jesus.

Is your next step apparent? If not, just choose one of these disciplines and start growing. Grow in your giving. Confess a sin. Write a song of praise.

Have you fallen down some steps? Maybe you even fell down seven steps. Get back up. Climb eight. The grace of God is coming to you through these written words.

Are you out of practice? It is easy to get comfortable. It can seem fun to set up camp once we have climbed a good amount of steps. Don't settle. God invites you to come ever closer. Get your eyes on Christ, not on comfort. Take your next step.

One last story: when I was 13 years old, I got lost in the wilderness far outside the city of Mazatlan, Mexico. After several hours, exposed to the hot summer sun, my skin was red, my lips were parched, and I was out of water. Eventually, I ended up on the right path that would lead to where I wanted to be: a place of friendship, refreshment, mission, and my trip's purpose. Desperately, I wanted to be there. I was weary. I was sore. I was frustrated. I fell down three times. My borrowed bike was useless. Instead of the bike carrying me, I was pushing it. What did I do? I didn't give up. (After all, here I am writing this to you.) No, I didn't give up. I didn't stop my journey. I took my next step. Then I took another step. Step by step I arrived at my destination.

Step by step, you will arrive at your destination. You will become the person that God destined you to be. You will become the person you desperately dream of.

Keep step with Jesus and you will get unstuck, restored, and renewed in faith, your spiritual life, and even in church.

Most importantly, you will become more like God.

MY PLAN TO KEEP GROWING TOWARDS JESUS

_____
_____
_____
_____
_____
_____
_____
_____
_____
_____
_____
_____
_____

TODAY'S DATE

_____

ACKNOWLEDGEMENTS

I want to thank the many, many people who have given me grace to grow. Life can be a roller coaster and three people stand out as people who gave me grace when I didn't deserve it.

TIMOTHY ACKER:

Dad, you are my hero. I've watched you all my life. I've seen you at your best and your worst. I watched you when we lost mom in a car accident. I watched you transition jobs. I watched you navigate the messiness of mission life in Mexico. We joke that I have watched the many different stages of *Tim*. More than any of the lessons you imparted, I thank you for modeling what it means to try to keep in step with God. I also appreciate that you haven't been perfect. That used to irritate me! But now, I understand. Life is unpredictable. Even in all that change, you have loved me, prayed for me, and encouraged me. Thank you.

TONY CLOUD:

Thank you. It's amazing that you were only thirty-five years old when you hired me for my first full-time pastoral position. Full of myself, I thought that *you* were the lucky one. After all, I thought I was pretty good! As I look back on our years together, I am so grateful that I had you to befriend me, mentor me, and give me grace. You provided me with opportunities to succeed and to fail. Thank you for loving *me* and not just loving what I could achieve.

TAYLOR ACKER:

Honey, thank you. I have come to realize that I can be a hard person to live with! I constantly have new things I want to do, my mind is always turning, I mis-communicate, I can get very frustrated at changes in plans, and I can easily be focused on what I want instead of what you need. After a decade together, we are still learning and still growing. So much of what we have achieved together is the grace you have provided me. Thank you for loving me and not a perfect version of what a husband should be.

ABOUT MIKE ACKER

Born to a drug smuggler and a witch, Mike Acker's parents experienced a radical change when they decided to become Christians by putting their trust in Jesus.

As a kid, the Ackers obeyed Jesus' command to love and serve people. They served the elderly in nursing homes, the homeless in Seattle soup kitchens, and people affected by AIDS in the 1980s. This compulsion to serve people in the name of Jesus caused the Ackers to move to Mexico in 1990. Mike Acker joined his family in taking care of the kids, feeding the hungry, building homes, and teaching people about the love of God.

After a year of intense wrestling with God, Mike embraced the path to becoming a Pastor. Internships, training, and university led to becoming a pastor to kids in 2000 while in college and then an associate pastor at the age of twenty-two. After nearly two decades of vocational ministry, Mike and Taylor decided to take a break from working in the church. Since then, he has embraced consultative sales, keynote speaking, coaching, authoring, and being available to watch the Seahawks on Sundays.

Mike continues to serve the poor and disenfranchised by giving and leading through an international non-profit, GO ON THE MISSION (https://www.goonthemission.com). In his role as Chairman of the Board, he has worked with the paid staff, the board of directors, the international staff as they collaborate to sponsor families, start schools, and build dozens of feeding centers.

Mike also enjoys watching America's Got Talent with his wife, Taylor; skiing with family; wrestling with his son; and going on adventures with his family.

BOOK MIKE ACKER TO SPEAK!

Book **Mike** for your church event or as your Keynote Speaker and you're guaranteed to make your event meaningful and memorable!

For two decades, Mike Acker has been speaking and preaching to audiences of 10 to 10,000. His unique style combines incredible stories, in-depth Biblical insights, and stand-up comedy style delivery. Mike empowers his audience with actionable truth to take their next on their journey in life.

> "Mike is the kind of leader who not only succeeds but understands why he succeeds. His gift in speaking is understanding what is actually going on in any given situation helping to identify the remedies and the reasons that will clear the obstacles and secure success. Mike genuinely cares."
> — **Daren Lindley, Good Catch Publishing**

> "Mike has an exceptional ability to combine both relational savvy with solid teaching. I have grown personally, professionally and in many other ways under his speaking and coaching. If you have the ability to hire Mike, do it. Your return on investment will not disappoint."
> — **Matthew Barnett, Citipoint Church**

For more info - **visit www.MikeAcker.com**

DO YOU WANT MORE?

Thank you for your interest!

I always have something new I'm working on. Sign up for my mailing list to get access to my leadership and communication articles. Along with new book releases, programs, and discounts!

TO GET STARTED, GO TO:

https://subscribe.stepstoadvance.com/me

SOMEONE NEEDS THIS BOOK. CAN YOU HELP?

If you liked this book and found it helpful, could you please take a brief moment to review it on Amazon?

Simply visit https://www.amazon.com/author/mikeacker to select *Grow Your Soul*. Then leave your honest feedback.

Your reviews help others see if this book can help them as well.

www.ingramcontent.com/pod-product-compliance
Lightning Source LLC
Chambersburg PA
CBHW071227080526
44587CB00013BA/1524